PRIDE AND PREJUDICE

Jane Austen

SPARK PUBLISHING

Spark Publishing
A Division of Barnes & Noble
120 Fifth Avenue
New York, NY 10011
www.sparknotes.com

ISBN-13: 978-1-4114-0328-4
ISBN-10: 1-4114-0328-2

Please submit changes or report errors to www.sparknotes.com/errors.

Printed in the United States.

10 9 8 7 6 5 4 3 2 1

Contents

CONTEXT

JANE AUSTEN WAS BORN in Steventon, England, in 1775, where she lived for the first twenty-five years of her life. Her father, George Austen, was the rector of the local parish and taught her largely at home. She began to write while in her teens and completed the original manuscript of *Pride and Prejudice*, titled *First Impressions*, between 1796 and 1797. A publisher rejected the manuscript, and it was not until 1809 that Austen began the revisions that would bring it to its final form. *Pride and Prejudice* was published in January 1813, two years after *Sense and Sensibility*, her first novel, and it achieved a popularity that has endured to this day. Austen published four more novels: *Mansfield Park, Emma, Northanger Abbey,* and *Persuasion*. The last two were published in 1818, a year after her death.

During Austen's life, however, only her immediate family knew of her authorship of these novels. At one point, she wrote behind a door that creaked when visitors approached; this warning allowed her to hide manuscripts before anyone could enter. Though publishing anonymously prevented her from acquiring an authorial reputation, it also enabled her to preserve her privacy at a time when English society associated a female's entrance into the public sphere with a reprehensible loss of femininity. Additionally, Austen may have sought anonymity because of the more general atmosphere of repression pervading her era. As the Napoleonic Wars (1800–1815) threatened the safety of monarchies throughout Europe, government censorship of literature proliferated.

The social milieu of Austen's Regency England was particularly stratified, and class divisions were rooted in family connections and wealth. In her work, Austen is often critical of the assumptions and prejudices of upper-class England. She distinguishes between internal merit (goodness of person) and external merit (rank and possessions). Though she frequently satirizes snobs, she also pokes fun at the poor breeding and misbehavior of those lower on the social scale. Nevertheless, Austen was in many ways a realist, and the England she depicts is one in which social mobility is limited and class-consciousness is strong.

Socially regimented ideas of appropriate behavior for each gender factored into Austen's work as well. While social advancement for young men lay in the military, church, or law, the chief method of self-improvement for women was the acquisition of wealth. Women could only accomplish this goal through successful marriage, which explains the ubiquity of matrimony as a goal and topic of conversation in Austen's writing. Though young women of Austen's day had more freedom to choose their husbands than in the early eighteenth century, practical considerations continued to limit their options.

Even so, critics often accuse Austen of portraying a limited world. As a clergyman's daughter, Austen would have done parish work and was certainly aware of the poor around her. However, she wrote about her own world, not theirs. The critiques she makes of class structure seem to include only the middle class and upper class; the lower classes, if they appear at all, are generally servants who seem perfectly pleased with their lot. This lack of interest in the lives of the poor may be a failure on Austen's part, but it should be understood as a failure shared by almost all of English society at the time.

In general, Austen occupies a curious position between the eighteenth and nineteenth centuries. Her favorite writer, whom she often quotes in her novels, was Dr. Samuel Johnson, the great model of eighteenth-century classicism and reason. Her plots, which often feature characters forging their respective ways through an established and rigid social hierarchy, bear similarities to such works of Johnson's contemporaries as Pamela, written by Samuel Richardson. Austen's novels also display an ambiguity about emotion and an appreciation for intelligence and natural beauty that aligns them with Romanticism. In their awareness of the conditions of modernity and city life and the consequences for family structure and individual characters, they prefigure much Victorian literature (as does her usage of such elements as frequent formal social gatherings, sketchy characters, and scandal).

Plot Overview

THE NEWS THAT A WEALTHY YOUNG GENTLEMAN named Charles Bingley has rented the manor of Netherfield Park causes a great stir in the nearby village of Longbourn, especially in the Bennet household. The Bennets have five unmarried daughters—from oldest to youngest, Jane, Elizabeth, Mary, Kitty, and Lydia—and Mrs. Bennet is desperate to see them all married. After Mr. Bennet pays a social visit to Mr. Bingley, the Bennets attend a ball at which Mr. Bingley is present. He is taken with Jane and spends much of the evening dancing with her. His close friend, Mr. Darcy, is less pleased with the evening and haughtily refuses to dance with Elizabeth, which makes everyone view him as arrogant and obnoxious.

At social functions over subsequent weeks, however, Mr. Darcy finds himself increasingly attracted to Elizabeth's charm and intelligence. Jane's friendship with Mr. Bingley also continues to burgeon, and Jane pays a visit to the Bingley mansion. On her journey to the house she is caught in a downpour and catches ill, forcing her to stay at Netherfield for several days. In order to tend to Jane, Elizabeth hikes through muddy fields and arrives with a spattered dress, much to the disdain of the snobbish Miss Bingley, Charles Bingley's sister. Miss Bingley's spite only increases when she notices that Darcy, whom she is pursuing, pays quite a bit of attention to Elizabeth.

When Elizabeth and Jane return home, they find Mr. Collins visiting their household. Mr. Collins is a young clergyman who stands to inherit Mr. Bennet's property, which has been "entailed," meaning that it can only be passed down to male heirs. Mr. Collins is a pompous fool, though he is quite enthralled by the Bennet girls. Shortly after his arrival, he makes a proposal of marriage to Elizabeth. She turns him down, wounding his pride. Meanwhile, the Bennet girls have become friendly with militia officers stationed in a nearby town. Among them is Wickham, a handsome young soldier who is friendly toward Elizabeth and tells her how Darcy cruelly cheated him out of an inheritance.

At the beginning of winter, the Bingleys and Darcy leave Netherfield and return to London, much to Jane's dismay. A further shock arrives with the news that Mr. Collins has become engaged to Charlotte Lucas, Elizabeth's best friend and the poor daughter of a local knight. Charlotte explains to Elizabeth that she is getting older and needs the match for financial reasons. Charlotte and Mr. Collins get married and Elizabeth promises to visit them at their new home. As winter progresses, Jane visits the city to see friends (hoping also that she might see Mr. Bingley). However, Miss Bingley visits her and behaves rudely, while Mr. Bingley fails to visit her at all. The marriage prospects for the Bennet girls appear bleak.

That spring, Elizabeth visits Charlotte, who now lives near the home of Mr. Collins's patron, Lady Catherine de Bourgh, who is also Darcy's aunt. Darcy calls on Lady Catherine and encounters Elizabeth, whose presence leads him to make a number of visits to the Collins's home, where she is staying. One day, he makes a shocking proposal of marriage, which Elizabeth quickly refuses. She tells Darcy that she considers him arrogant and unpleasant, then scolds him for steering Bingley away from Jane and disinheriting Wickham. Darcy leaves her but shortly thereafter delivers a letter to her. In this letter, he admits that he urged Bingley to distance himself from Jane, but claims he did so only because he thought their romance was not serious. As for Wickham, he informs Elizabeth that the young officer is a liar and that the real cause of their disagreement was Wickham's attempt to elope with his young sister, Georgiana Darcy.

This letter causes Elizabeth to reevaluate her feelings about Darcy. She returns home and acts coldly toward Wickham. The militia is leaving town, which makes the younger, rather man-crazy Bennet girls distraught. Lydia manages to obtain permission from her father to spend the summer with an old colonel in Brighton, where Wickham's regiment will be stationed. With the arrival of June, Elizabeth goes on another journey, this time with the Gardiners, who are relatives of the Bennets. The trip takes her to the North and eventually to the neighborhood of Pemberley, Darcy's estate. She visits Pemberley, after making sure that Darcy is away, and delights in the building and grounds, while hearing from Darcy's servants that he is a wonderful, generous master. Suddenly, Darcy arrives and behaves cordially toward her. Making no mention of his proposal, he entertains the Gardiners and invites Elizabeth to meet his sister.

Shortly thereafter, however, a letter arrives from home, telling Elizabeth that Lydia has eloped with Wickham and that the couple is nowhere to be found, which suggests that they may be living together out of wedlock. Fearful of the disgrace such a situation would bring on her entire family, Elizabeth hastens home. Mr. Gardiner and Mr. Bennet go off to search for Lydia, but Mr. Bennet eventually returns home empty-handed. Just when all hope seems lost, a letter comes from Mr. Gardiner saying that the couple has been found and that Wickham has agreed to marry Lydia in exchange for an annual income. The Bennets are convinced that Mr. Gardiner has paid off Wickham, but Elizabeth learns that the source of the money, and of her family's salvation, was none other than Darcy.

Now married, Wickham and Lydia return to Longbourn briefly, where Mr. Bennet treats them coldly. They then depart for Wickham's new assignment in the North of England. Shortly thereafter, Bingley returns to Netherfield and resumes his courtship of Jane. Darcy goes to stay with him and pays visits to the Bennets but makes no mention of his desire to marry Elizabeth. Bingley, on the other hand, presses his suit and proposes to Jane, to the delight of everyone but Bingley's haughty sister. While the family celebrates, Lady Catherine de Bourgh pays a visit to Longbourn. She corners Elizabeth and says that she has heard that Darcy, her nephew, is planning to marry her. Since she considers a Bennet an unsuitable match for a Darcy, Lady Catherine demands that Elizabeth promise to refuse him. Elizabeth spiritedly refuses, saying she is not engaged to Darcy, but she will not promise anything against her own happiness. A little later, Elizabeth and Darcy go out walking together and he tells her that his feelings have not altered since the spring. She tenderly accepts his proposal, and both Jane and Elizabeth are married.

CHARACTER LIST

Elizabeth Bennet The novel's protagonist. The second daughter
of Mr. Bennet, Elizabeth is the most intelligent and
sensible of the five Bennet sisters. She is well read and
quick-witted, with a tongue that occasionally proves
too sharp for her own good. Her realization of Darcy's
essential goodness eventually triumphs over her initial
prejudice against him.

Fitzwilliam Darcy A wealthy gentleman, the master of Pemberley,
and the nephew of Lady Catherine de Bourgh. Though
Darcy is intelligent and honest, his excess of pride
causes him to look down on his social inferiors.
Over the course of the novel, he tempers his class-
consciousness and learns to admire and love Elizabeth
for her strong character.

Jane Bennet The eldest and most beautiful Bennet sister. Jane is
more reserved and gentler than Elizabeth. The easy
pleasantness with which she and Bingley interact
contrasts starkly with the mutual distaste that marks
the encounters between Elizabeth and Darcy.

Charles Bingley Darcy's considerably wealthy best friend.
Bingley's purchase of Netherfield, an estate near the
Bennets, serves as the impetus for the novel. He is a
genial, well-intentioned gentleman, whose easygoing
nature contrasts with Darcy's initially discourteous
demeanor. He is blissfully uncaring about class
differences.

Mr. Bennet The patriarch of the Bennet family, a gentleman of
modest income with five unmarried daughters. Mr.
Bennet has a sarcastic, cynical sense of humor that he
uses to purposefully irritate his wife. Though he loves
his daughters (Elizabeth in particular), he often fails

as a parent, preferring to withdraw from the never-ending marriage concerns of the women around him rather than offer help.

Mrs. Bennet Mr. Bennet's wife, a foolish, noisy woman whose only goal in life is to see her daughters married. Because of her low breeding and often unbecoming behavior, Mrs. Bennet often repels the very suitors whom she tries to attract for her daughters.

George Wickham A handsome, fortune-hunting militia officer. Wickham's good looks and charm attract Elizabeth initially, but Darcy's revelation about Wickham's disreputable past clues her in to his true nature and simultaneously draws her closer to Darcy.

Lydia Bennet The youngest Bennet sister, she is gossipy, immature, and self-involved. Unlike Elizabeth, Lydia flings herself headlong into romance and ends up running off with Wickham.

Mr. Collins A pompous, generally idiotic clergyman who stands to inherit Mr. Bennet's property. Mr. Collins's own social status is nothing to brag about, but he takes great pains to let everyone and anyone know that Lady Catherine de Bourgh serves as his patroness. He is the worst combination of snobbish and obsequious.

Miss Bingley Bingley's snobbish sister. Miss Bingley bears inordinate disdain for Elizabeth's middle-class background. Her vain attempts to garner Darcy's attention cause Darcy to admire Elizabeth's self-possessed character even more.

Lady Catherine de Bourgh A rich, bossy noblewoman; Mr. Collins's patron and Darcy's aunt. Lady Catherine epitomizes class snobbery, especially in her attempts to order the middle-class Elizabeth away from her well-bred nephew.

Mr. and Mrs. Gardiner Mrs. Bennet's brother and his wife. The Gardiners, caring, nurturing, and full of common sense, often prove to be better parents to the Bennet daughters than Mr. Bennet and his wife.

Charlotte Lucas Elizabeth's dear friend. Pragmatic where Elizabeth is romantic, and also six years older than Elizabeth, Charlotte does not view love as the most vital component of a marriage. She is more interested in having a comfortable home. Thus, when Mr. Collins proposes, she accepts.

Georgiana Darcy Darcy's sister. She is immensely pretty and just as shy. She has great skill at playing the pianoforte.

Mary Bennet The middle Bennet sister, bookish and pedantic.

Catherine Bennet The fourth Bennet sister. Like Lydia, she is girlishly enthralled with the soldiers.

CHARACTER LIST

ANALYSIS OF MAJOR CHARACTERS

ELIZABETH BENNET

The second daughter in the Bennet family, and the most intelligent and quick-witted, Elizabeth is the protagonist of *Pride and Prejudice* and one of the most well-known female characters in English literature. Her admirable qualities are numerous—she is lovely, clever, and, in a novel defined by dialogue, she converses as brilliantly as anyone. Her honesty, virtue, and lively wit enable her to rise above the nonsense and bad behavior that pervade her class-bound and often spiteful society. Nevertheless, her sharp tongue and tendency to make hasty judgments often lead her astray; *Pride and Prejudice* is essentially the story of how she (and her true love, Darcy) overcome all obstacles—including their own personal failings—to find romantic happiness. Elizabeth must not only cope with a hopeless mother, a distant father, two badly behaved younger siblings, and several snobbish, antagonizing females, she must also overcome her own mistaken impressions of Darcy, which initially lead her to reject his proposals of marriage. Her charms are sufficient to keep him interested, fortunately, while she navigates familial and social turmoil. As she gradually comes to recognize the nobility of Darcy's character, she realizes the error of her initial prejudice against him.

FITZWILLIAM DARCY

The son of a wealthy, well-established family and the master of the great estate of Pemberley, Darcy is Elizabeth's male counterpart. The narrator relates Elizabeth's point of view of events more often than Darcy's, so Elizabeth often seems a more sympathetic figure. The reader eventually realizes, however, that Darcy is her ideal match. Intelligent and forthright, he too has a tendency to judge too hastily and harshly, and his high birth and wealth make him overly proud and overly conscious of his social status. Indeed, his haughtiness makes him initially bungle his courtship. When he proposes to her, for instance, he dwells more on how unsuitable a match she is than on her charms, beauty, or anything else complimentary. Her rejection of his advances builds a kind of humility in him. Darcy demonstrates his continued devotion to Elizabeth, in spite of his distaste for her low connections, when he rescues Lydia and the entire Bennet family from disgrace, and when he goes against the wishes of his haughty aunt, Lady Catherine de Bourgh, by continuing to pursue Elizabeth. Darcy proves himself worthy of Elizabeth, and she ends up repenting her earlier, overly harsh judgment of him.

JANE BENNET AND CHARLES BINGLEY

Elizabeth's beautiful elder sister and Darcy's wealthy best friend, Jane and Bingley engage in a courtship that occupies a central place in the novel. They first meet at the ball in Meryton and enjoy an immediate mutual attraction. They are spoken of as a potential couple throughout the book, long before anyone imagines that Darcy and Elizabeth might marry. Despite their centrality to the narrative, they are vague characters, sketched by Austen rather than carefully drawn. Indeed, they are so similar in nature and behavior that they can be described together: both are cheerful, friendly, and good-natured, always ready to think the best of others; they lack entirely the prickly egotism of Elizabeth and Darcy. Jane's gentle spirit serves as a foil for her sister's fiery, contentious nature, while Bingley's eager friendliness contrasts with Darcy's stiff pride. Their principal characteristics are goodwill and compatibility, and the contrast of their romance with that of Darcy and Elizabeth is remarkable. Jane and Bingley exhibit to the reader true love unhampered by either pride or prejudice, though in their simple goodness, they also demonstrate that such a love is mildly dull.

MR. BENNET

Mr. Bennet is the patriarch of the Bennet household—the husband of Mrs. Bennet and the father of Jane, Elizabeth, Lydia, Kitty, and Mary. He is a man driven to exasperation by his ridiculous wife and difficult daughters. He reacts by withdrawing from his family and assuming a detached attitude punctuated by bursts of sarcastic humor. He is closest to Elizabeth because they are the two most intelligent Bennets. Initially, his dry wit and self-possession in the face of his wife's hysteria make him a sympathetic figure, but, though he remains likable throughout, the reader gradually loses respect for him as it becomes clear that the price of his detachment is considerable.

Detached from his family, he is a weak father and, at critical moments, fails his family. In particular, his foolish indulgence of Lydia's immature behavior nearly leads to general disgrace when she elopes with Wickham. Further, upon her disappearance, he proves largely ineffective. It is left to Mr. Gardiner and Darcy to track Lydia down and rectify the situation. Ultimately, Mr. Bennet would rather withdraw from the world than cope with it.

MRS. BENNET

Mrs. Bennet is a miraculously tiresome character. Noisy and foolish, she is a woman consumed by the desire to see her daughters married and seems to care for nothing else in the world. Ironically, her single-minded pursuit of this goal tends to backfire, as her lack of social graces alienates the very people (Darcy and Bingley) whom she tries desperately to attract. Austen uses her continually to highlight the necessity of marriage for young women. Mrs. Bennet also serves as a middle-class counterpoint to such upper-class snobs as Lady Catherine and Miss Bingley, demonstrating that foolishness can be found at every level of society. In the end, however, Mrs. Bennet proves such an unattractive figure, lacking redeeming characteristics of any kind, that some readers have accused Austen of unfairness in portraying her—as if Austen, like Mr. Bennet, took perverse pleasure in poking fun at a woman already scorned as a result of her ill breeding.

THEMES, MOTIFS & SYMBOLS

THEMES

Themes are the fundamental and often universal ideas explored in a literary work.

LOVE
Pride and Prejudice contains one of the most cherished love stories in English literature: the courtship between Darcy and Elizabeth. As in any good love story, the lovers must elude and overcome numerous stumbling blocks, beginning with the tensions caused by the lovers' own personal qualities. Elizabeth's pride makes her misjudge Darcy on the basis of a poor first impression, while Darcy's prejudice against Elizabeth's poor social standing blinds him, for a time, to her many virtues. (Of course, one could also say that Elizabeth is guilty of prejudice and Darcy of pride—the title cuts both ways.) Austen, meanwhile, poses countless smaller obstacles to the realization of the love between Elizabeth and Darcy, including Lady Catherine's attempt to control her nephew, Miss Bingley's snobbery, Mrs. Bennet's idiocy, and Wickham's deceit. In each case, anxieties about social connections, or the desire for better social connections, interfere with the workings of love. Darcy and Elizabeth's realization of a mutual and tender love seems to imply that Austen views love as something independent of these social forces, as something that can be captured if only an individual is able to escape the warping effects of hierarchical society. Austen does sound some more realist (or, one could say, cynical) notes about love, using the character of Charlotte Lucas, who marries the buffoon Mr. Collins for his money, to demonstrate that the heart does not always dictate marriage. Yet with her central characters, Austen suggests that true love is a force separate from society and one that can conquer even the most difficult of circumstances.

REPUTATION
Pride and Prejudice depicts a society in which a woman's reputation is of the utmost importance. A woman is expected to behave in

certain ways. Stepping outside the social norms makes her vulnerable to ostracism. This theme appears in the novel, when Elizabeth walks to Netherfield and arrives with muddy skirts, to the shock of the reputation-conscious Miss Bingley and her friends. At other points, the ill-mannered, ridiculous behavior of Mrs. Bennet gives her a bad reputation with the more refined (and snobbish) Darcys and Bingleys. Austen pokes gentle fun at the snobs in these examples, but later in the novel, when Lydia elopes with Wickham and lives with him out of wedlock, the author treats reputation as a very serious matter. By becoming Wickham's lover without benefit of marriage, Lydia clearly places herself outside the social pale, and her disgrace threatens the entire Bennet family. The fact that Lydia's judgment, however terrible, would likely have condemned the other Bennet sisters to marriageless lives seems grossly unfair. Why should Elizabeth's reputation suffer along with Lydia's? Darcy's intervention on the Bennets' behalf thus becomes all the more generous, but some readers might resent that such an intervention was necessary at all. If Darcy's money had failed to convince Wickham to marry Lydia, would Darcy have still married Elizabeth? Does his transcendence of prejudice extend that far? The happy ending of *Pride and Prejudice* is certainly emotionally satisfying, but in many ways it leaves the theme of reputation, and the importance placed on reputation, unexplored. One can ask of *Pride and Prejudice*, to what extent does it critique social structures, and to what extent does it simply accept their inevitability?

CLASS

The theme of class is related to reputation, in that both reflect the strictly regimented nature of life for the middle and upper classes in Regency England. The lines of class are strictly drawn. While the Bennets, who are middle class, may socialize with the upper-class Bingleys and Darcys, they are clearly their social inferiors and are treated as such. Austen satirizes this kind of class-consciousness, particularly in the character of Mr. Collins, who spends most of his time toadying to his upper-class patron, Lady Catherine de Bourgh. Though Mr. Collins offers an extreme example, he is not the only one to hold such views. His conception of the importance of class is shared, among others, by Mr. Darcy, who believes in the dignity of his lineage; Miss Bingley, who dislikes anyone not as socially accepted as she is; and Wickham, who will do anything he can to get enough money to raise himself into a higher station. Mr. Collins's views are merely the most extreme and obvious. The satire directed at Mr. Collins is therefore also more subtly directed at the entire social hierarchy and the conception of all those within it at its correctness, in complete disregard of other, more worthy virtues. Through the Darcy-Elizabeth and Bingley-Jane marriages, Austen shows the power of love and happiness to overcome class boundaries and prejudices, thereby implying that such prejudices are hollow, unfeeling, and unproductive. Of course, this whole discussion of class must be made with the understanding that Austen herself is often criticized as being a classist: she doesn't really represent anyone from the lower classes; those servants she does portray are generally happy with their lot. Austen does criticize class structure but only a limited slice of that structure.

MOTIFS

Motifs are recurring structures, contrasts, and literary devices that can help to develop and inform the text's major themes.

COURTSHIP

In a sense, *Pride and Prejudice* is the story of two courtships—those between Darcy and Elizabeth and between Bingley and Jane. Within this broad structure appear other, smaller courtships: Mr. Collins's aborted wooing of Elizabeth, followed by his successful wooing of Charlotte Lucas; Miss Bingley's unsuccessful attempt to attract Darcy; Wickham's pursuit first of Elizabeth, then of the never-seen Miss King, and finally of Lydia. Courtship therefore takes on a profound, if often unspoken, importance in the novel. Marriage is the ultimate goal, courtship constitutes the real working-out of love. Courtship becomes a sort of forge of a person's personality, and each courtship becomes a microcosm for different sorts of love (or different ways to abuse love as a means to social advancement).

JOURNEYS

Nearly every scene in *Pride and Prejudice* takes place indoors, and the action centers around the Bennet home in the small village of Longbourn. Nevertheless, journeys—even short ones—function repeatedly as catalysts for change in the novel. Elizabeth's first journey, by which she intends simply to visit Charlotte and Mr. Collins, brings her into contact with Mr. Darcy, and leads to his first proposal. Her second journey takes her to Derby and Pemberley, where she fans the growing flame of her affection for Darcy. The third journey, meanwhile, sends various people in pursuit of Wickham and Lydia, and the journey ends with Darcy tracking them down and saving the Bennet family honor, in the process demonstrating his continued devotion to Elizabeth.

SYMBOLS

Symbols are objects, characters, figures, and colors used to represent abstract ideas or concepts.

PEMBERLEY

Pride and Prejudice is remarkably free of explicit symbolism, which perhaps has something to do with the novel's reliance on dialogue over description. Nevertheless, Pemberley, Darcy's estate, sits at the center of the novel, literally and figuratively, as a geographic symbol of the man who owns it. Elizabeth visits it at a time when her feelings toward Darcy are beginning to warm; she is enchanted by its beauty and charm, and by the picturesque countryside, just as she will be charmed, increasingly, by the gifts of its owner. Austen makes the connection explicit when she describes the stream that flows beside the mansion. "In front," she writes, "a stream of some natural importance was swelled into greater, but without any artificial appearance." Darcy possesses a "natural importance" that is "swelled" by his arrogance, but which coexists with a genuine honesty and lack of "artificial appearance." Like the stream, he is neither "formal, nor falsely adorned." Pemberley even offers a symbol-within-a-symbol for their budding romance: when Elizabeth encounters Darcy on the estate, she is crossing a small bridge, suggesting the broad gulf of misunderstanding and class prejudice that lies between them—and the bridge that their love will build across it.

SUMMARY & ANALYSIS

CHAPTERS 1–4

SUMMARY: CHAPTERS 1–2

> *It is a truth universally acknowledged, that a single man in possession of a good fortune, must be in want of a wife.*
>
> *(See* QUOTATIONS, *p. 51)*

The news that a wealthy young gentleman named Charles Bingley has rented the manor known as Netherfield Park causes a great stir in the neighboring village of Longbourn, especially in the Bennet household. The Bennets have five unmarried daughters, and Mrs. Bennet, a foolish and fussy gossip, is the sort who agrees with the novel's opening words: "It is a truth universally acknowledged, that a single man in possession of a good fortune, must be in want of a wife." She sees Bingley's arrival as an opportunity for one of the girls to obtain a wealthy spouse, and she therefore insists that her husband call on the new arrival immediately. Mr. Bennet torments his family by pretending to have no interest in doing so, but he eventually meets with Mr. Bingley without their knowing. When he reveals to Mrs. Bennet and his daughters that he has made their new neighbor's acquaintance, they are overjoyed and excited.

SUMMARY: CHAPTERS 3–4

> *She is tolerable; but not handsome enough to tempt me.*
>
> *(See* QUOTATIONS, *p. 52)*

Eager to learn more, Mrs. Bennet and the girls question Mr. Bennet incessantly. A few days later, Mr. Bingley returns the visit, though he does not meet Mr. Bennet's daughters. The Bennets invite him to dinner shortly afterward, but he is called away to London. Soon, however, he returns to Netherfield Park with his two sisters, his brother-in-law, and a friend named Darcy.

Mr. Bingley and his guests go to a ball in the nearby town of Meryton. The Bennet sisters attend the ball with their mother. The eldest daughter, Jane, dances twice with Bingley. Within Elizabeth's hearing, Bingley exclaims to Darcy that Jane is "the most beautiful creature" he has ever beheld. Bingley suggests that Darcy dance with Elizabeth, but Darcy refuses, saying, "she is tolerable, but not handsome enough to tempt me." He proceeds to declare that he has no interest in women who are "slighted by other men." Elizabeth takes an immediate and understandable disliking to Darcy. Because of Darcy's comments and refusal to dance with anyone not rich and well bred, the neighborhood takes a similar dislike; it declares Bingley, on the other hand, to be quite "amiable."

At the end of the evening, the Bennet women return to their house, where Mrs. Bennet regales her husband with stories from the evening until he insists that she be silent. Upstairs, Jane relates to Elizabeth her surprise that Bingley danced with her twice, and Elizabeth replies that Jane is unaware of her own beauty. Both girls agree that Bingley's sisters are not well-mannered, but whereas Jane insists that they are charming in close conversation, Elizabeth continues to harbor a dislike for them.

The narrator then provides the reader with Bingley's background: he inherited a hundred thousand pounds from his father, but for now, in spite of his sisters' complaints, he lives as a tenant. His friendship with Darcy is "steady," despite the contrast in their characters, illustrated in their respective reactions to the Meryton ball. Bingley, cheerful and sociable, has an excellent time and is taken with Jane; Darcy, more clever but less tactful, finds the people dull and even criticizes Jane for smiling too often (Bingley's sisters, on the other hand, find Jane to be "a sweet girl," and Bingley therefore feels secure in his good opinion of her).

ANALYSIS: CHAPTERS 1–4

The opening sentence of *Pride and Prejudice*—"It is a truth universally acknowledged, that a single man in possession of a good fortune, must be in want of a wife"—establishes the centrality of advantageous marriage, a fundamental social value of Regency England. The arrival of Mr. Bingley (and news of his fortune) is the event that sets the novel in motion. He delivers the prospect of a marriage of wealth and good connections for the eager Bennet girls. The opening sentence has a subtle, unstated significance. In its declarative and hopeful claim that a wealthy man must be looking for a wife, it hides beneath its surface the truth of such matters: a single woman must be in want of a husband, especially a wealthy one.

The first chapter consists almost entirely of dialogue, a typical instance of Austen's technique of using the manner in which characters express themselves to reveal their traits and attitudes. Its last paragraph, in which the narrator describes Mr. Bennet as a "mixture of quick parts, sarcastic humour, reserve, and caprice," and his wife as "a woman of mean understanding, little information, and uncertain temper," simply confirms the character assessments that the reader has already made based on their conversation: Mrs. Bennett embodies ill breeding and is prone to monotone hysteria; Mr. Bennet is a wit who retreats from his wife's overly serious demeanor. There is little physical description of the characters in *Pride and Prejudice*, so the reader's perception of them is shaped largely by their words. Darcy makes the importance of the verbal explicit at the end of the novel when he tells Elizabeth that he was first attracted to her by "the liveliness of [her] mind."

The ball at Meryton is important to the structure of the novel since it brings the two couples—Darcy and Elizabeth, Bingley and Jane—together for the first time. Austen's original title for the novel was *First Impressions,* and these individuals' first impressions at the ball initiate the contrasting patterns of the two principal male-female relationships. The relative effortlessness with which Bingley and Jane interact is indicative of their easygoing natures; the obstacles that the novel places in the way of their happiness are in no way caused by Jane or Bingley themselves. Indeed, their feelings for one another seem to change little after the initial attraction—there is no development of their love, only the delay of its consummation. Darcy's bad behavior, on the other hand, immediately betrays the pride and sense of social superiority that will most hinder him from finding his way to Elizabeth. His snub of her creates a mutual dislike, in contrast to the mutual attraction between Jane and Bingley. Further, while Darcy's opinion of Elizabeth changes within a few chapters, her (and the reader's) sense of him as self-important and arrogant remains unaltered until midway through the novel.

CHAPTERS 5–8

SUMMARY: CHAPTERS 5–6

The Bennets' neighbors are Sir William Lucas, his wife, and their children. The eldest of these children, Charlotte, is Elizabeth's closest friend. The morning after the ball, the women of the two families discuss the evening. They decide that while Bingley danced with Charlotte first, he considered Jane to be the prettiest of the local girls. The discussion then turns to Mr. Darcy, and Elizabeth states that she will never dance with him; everyone agrees that Darcy, despite his family and fortune, is too proud to be likable.

Bingley's sisters exchange visits with the Bennets and attempt to befriend Elizabeth and Jane. Meanwhile, Bingley continues to pay attention to Jane, and Elizabeth decides that her sister is "in a way to be very much in love" with him but is concealing it very well. She discusses this with Charlotte Lucas, who comments that if Jane conceals it too well, Bingley may lose interest. Elizabeth says it is better for a young woman to be patient until she is sure of her feelings; Charlotte disagrees, saying that it is best not to know too much about the faults of one's future husband.

Darcy finds himself attracted to Elizabeth. He begins listening to her conversations at parties, much to her surprise. At one party at the Lucas house, Sir William attempts to persuade Elizabeth and Darcy to dance together, but Elizabeth refuses. Shortly afterward, Darcy tells Bingley's unmarried sister that "Miss Elizabeth Bennet" is now the object of his admiration.

Summary: Chapters 7–8

The reader learns that Mr. Bennet's property is entailed, meaning that it must pass to a man after Mr. Bennet's death and cannot be inherited by any of his daughters. His two youngest children, Catherine (nicknamed Kitty) and Lydia, entertain themselves by beginning a series of visits to their mother's sister, Mrs. Phillips, in the town of Meryton, and gossiping about the militia stationed there.

One night, while the Bennets are discussing the soldiers over dinner, a note arrives inviting Jane to Netherfield Park for a day. Mrs. Bennet conspires to send Jane by horse rather than coach, knowing that it will rain and that Jane will consequently have to spend the night at Mr. Bingley's house. Unfortunately, their plan works out too well: Jane is soaked, falls ill, and is forced to remain at Netherfield as an invalid. Elizabeth goes to visit her, hiking over on foot. When she arrives with soaked and dirty stockings she causes quite a stir and is certain that the Bingleys hold her in contempt for her soiled clothes. Jane insists that her sister spend the night, and the Bingleys consent.

That night, while Elizabeth visits Jane, the Bingley sisters poke fun at the Bennets. Darcy and Mr. Bingley defend them, though Darcy concedes, first, that he would not want his sister ever to go out on such a walking expedition and, second, that the Bennets' lack of wealth and family make them poor marriage prospects. When

Elizabeth returns to the room, the discussion turns to Darcy's library at his ancestral home of Pemberley and then to Darcy's opinions on what constitutes an "accomplished woman." After he and Bingley list the attributes that such a woman would possess, Elizabeth declares that she "never saw such capacity, and taste, and application, and elegance, as you describe, united," implying that Darcy is far too demanding.

Analysis: Chapters 5–8

The introduction of the Lucases allows Austen to comment on the pretensions that accompany social rank. Recently knighted, Sir William is described as having felt his new distinction "a little too strongly" and moved away from town in order to "think with pleasure of his own importance." Sir William remains a sympathetic figure despite his snobbery, but the same cannot be said of Bingley's sister, whose class-consciousness becomes increasingly evident. Awareness of class difference is a pressing reality in *Pride and Prejudice*. This awareness colors the attitudes that characters of different social status feel toward one another. This awareness cuts both ways: as Darcy and Elizabeth demonstrate, the well-born and the socially inferior prove equally likely to harbor prejudices that blind them to others' true natures.

Charlotte Lucas's observation that Jane does not display her affection for Bingley illuminates the careful structure of the novel. Darcy notices the same reticence in Jane, but he assumes that she is not in love with Bingley. Charlotte's conversation with Elizabeth, then, foreshadows Darcy's justification for separating Bingley from Jane. Similarly, the author prepares the reader for subsequent developments in other relationships: Charlotte's belief that it is better not to know one's husband too well foreshadows her "practical" marriage to Collins, while Elizabeth's more romantic view anticipates her refusal of two proposals that might have been accepted by others.

As in *Sense and Sensibility*, Austen emphasizes the matter of entailment in order to create a sense of urgency about the search for a husband. Though Jane is the eldest child in a fairly well-off family, her status as a woman precludes her from enjoying the success her father has experienced. When her father dies, the estate will turn over to Mr. Collins, the oldest male relative. The mention of entailment stresses not just the value society places on making a good marriage but also the way that the structures of society make a good marriage a prerequisite for a "good" life (the connotation of "good" being wealthy). Austen thus offers commentary on the plight of women. Through both law and prescribed gender roles, Austen's society leaves women few options for the advancement or betterment of their situations.

Language proves of central importance to relationships in *Pride and Prejudice,* as Austen uses conversation to reveal character. The interactions between Darcy and Elizabeth primarily take the forms of banter and argument, and Elizabeth's words provide Darcy access to a deeper aspect of her character, one that appeals to him and allows him to begin to move past his initial prejudice. While their disagreement over the possibility of a "perfect" woman reinforces his apparent egotism and self-absorption, it also gives Elizabeth a chance to shine in debate. Whereas she does not live up to Darcy's physical and social requirements for a perfect woman, she exceeds those concerning the "liveliness" of the perfect woman's mind.

The novel begins to undermine the reader's negative impression of Darcy by contrasting him with Miss Bingley. Though his arrogance remains unpleasant, he is unwilling to join in Miss Bingley's snobbish dismissals of Elizabeth and her family. Like Lady Catherine de Bourgh later on, Miss Bingley serves as the voice of "society," criticizing Elizabeth's middle-class status and lack of social connections. Also like Lady Catherine, her primary motivation is jealousy: just as Lady Catherine wants Darcy to marry her niece, Miss Bingley wants him for herself. Both women exhibit a spite colored by self-interest.

CHAPTERS 9–12

SUMMARY: CHAPTERS 9–10

The next day, Mrs. Bennet arrives with Lydia and Catherine to visit Jane. To Elizabeth's dismay, Mrs. Bennet spends much of her visit trying to convince Bingley to remain at Netherfield. During her stay, Mrs. Bennet makes a general fool of herself, first by comparing country life to the city and then by prattling on about Jane's beauty. Near the end of the visit, fifteen-year-old Lydia asks Bingley whether he will hold a ball at Netherfield Park. He replies that he must wait until Jane is fully recovered to hold a ball.

In the evening, Elizabeth observes Miss Bingley piling compliments upon Darcy as he writes to his sister. The conversation turns to Bingley's style of letter writing and then to Bingley's impetuous behavior, which entangles Elizabeth and Darcy in an argument over the virtues of accepting the advice of friends. Afterward, Miss Bingley plays "a lively Scotch air" on the pianoforte, and Elizabeth again refuses to dance with Darcy. Her refusal only increases his admiration, and he considers that "were it not for the inferiority of her connections, he should be in some danger." Miss Bingley, observing his attraction, becomes jealous and spends the following day making fun of Elizabeth's family, inviting Darcy to imagine them connected to his proud and respectable line.

That night, Miss Bingley begins reading in imitation of Darcy—a further attempt to impress him. She chooses her book merely because it is the second volume of the one that Darcy is reading. Of course, being uninterested in literature, she is quickly bored and says loudly, "I declare after all there is no enjoyment like reading! How much sooner one tires of any thing than of a book!—When I have a house of my own, I shall be miserable if I have not an excellent library."

Summary: Chapters 11–12

Miss Bingley spends the following night in similar fashion, trying to attract Darcy's attention: first by reading, then by criticizing the foolishness of balls, and finally by walking about the room. Only when she asks Elizabeth to walk with her, however, does Darcy look up, and then the two women discuss the possibility of finding something to ridicule in his character. He states that his only fault is resentment—"my good opinion once lost is lost forever." Elizabeth replies that it is hard to laugh at a "propensity to hate every body," and Miss Bingley, observing Elizabeth's monopolization of Darcy's attention once again, insists on music.

The next morning, Elizabeth writes to her mother to say that she and Jane are ready to return home. Mrs. Bennet wishes Jane to stay longer with Bingley, and she refuses to send the carriage. Elizabeth, anxious to be away, insists on borrowing Bingley's carriage and she and her sister leave Netherfield Park. Darcy is glad to see them go, as Elizabeth attracts him "more than he liked," considering her unsuitability as a prospect for matrimony.

Analysis: Chapters 9–12

The continuation of Elizabeth's visit to Netherfield accentuates the respective attitudes of Miss Bingley and Darcy toward their guest: jealousy on the part of the former, admiration on that of the latter.

Elizabeth poses a separate threat to each of them. Miss Bingley fears her as a rival for Darcy's affection, and Darcy fears that he will succumb to his growing attraction to her despite the impracticality of marriage to one of such inferior rank and family. The anxiety created by class-consciousness thereby becomes a self-perpetuating, warping institution. Darcy, concerned that he may affect his own reputation by linking it to the poor reputation of another, tries to avoid talking to Elizabeth entirely on the final day she spends at Netherfield. He must tie himself up in a sort of logical knot; class-consciousness transforms Elizabeth, who is perfect for him, as something to be feared. Miss Bingley demonstrates how, once a class system develops, it maintains its coherence. Miss Bingley feels threatened by Elizabeth and knows she cannot compete with Elizabeth on the basis of her virtues or talents. Her means of defense is to bring class-anxiety to bear; by the luck of her birth, Miss Bingley has been stamped as superior. She now uses the entire social institution of class to maintain her superiority, even though all logic and experience show that superiority to be a lie.

In these chapters, the narrator portrays Miss Bingley as Elizabeth's opposite—foolish where the heroine is quick-witted, desperate for Darcy's attention while Elizabeth disdains him. Bingley's sister spends her energy attempting to conform to what she perceives to be Darcy's idea of a perfect woman. Her embarrassingly obvious flirtation makes her a figure of amusement for the reader—she is a parody of the man-hungry, snobbish, upper-class woman. By toadying up to Darcy, she ends up losing him to Elizabeth, despite the fact that Elizabeth does not make any attempt to appeal to him. By showing Miss Bingley as a scheming rival for Darcy's love whose tactics are uninspired, the novel highlights Elizabeth's originality and independence of spirit, and suggests that these, not the laundry list of accomplishments that Darcy gives, are the qualities that Darcy truly desires in a woman. His rejection of Miss Bingley's advances, then, serves to improve the reader's opinion of Darcy, as his ability to admire a social inferior separates him from ultra-elitist snobs such as Miss Bingley.

CHAPTERS 13–17

SUMMARY: CHAPTERS 13–15

The morning after his daughters return from Netherfield, Mr. Bennet informs his wife of an imminent visit from a Mr. William Collins, who will inherit Mr. Bennet's property. Mr. Collins, the reader learns from a letter he sends to the Bennets, is a clergyman whom the wealthy noblewoman Lady Catherine de Bourgh has recently selected to serve her parish. His letter, as Mr. Bennet puts it, contains "a mixture of servility and self-importance," and his personality is similar. He arrives at Longbourn and apologizes for being entitled to the Bennets' property but spends much of his time admiring and complimenting the house that will one day be his.

At dinner, Mr. Collins lavishes praise on Lady Catherine de Bourgh and her daughter, a lovely invalid who will one day inherit the de Bourgh fortune. After the meal, he is asked to read to the girls, but he refuses to read a novel and reads from a book of sermons instead. Lydia becomes so bored that she interrupts his reading with more gossip about the soldiers. Mr. Collins is offended and abandons the reading, choosing to play backgammon with Mr. Bennet.

Mr. Collins is in search of a wife and when Mrs. Bennet hints that Jane may soon be engaged, he fixes his attention on Elizabeth. The day after his arrival, he accompanies the sisters to the town of Meryton, where they encounter one of Lydia's officer friends, Mr. Denny. Denny introduces his friend, Mr. Wickham, who has just joined the militia, and the young women find Wickham charming. While they converse, Darcy and Bingley happen by, and Elizabeth notices that Wickham and Darcy are extremely cold to each other.

Darcy and Bingley depart, and the company pays a visit to Mrs. Phillips, Mrs. Bennet's sister, who invites the Bennets and Mr. Collins to dine at her house the following night. The girls convince her to invite Wickham as well. They return home and Mr. Collins spends the evening telling Mrs. Bennet how greatly her sister's good breeding impresses him.

SUMMARY: CHAPTERS 16–17

At the Phillips's dinner party, Wickham proves the center of attention and Mr. Collins fades into the background. Eventually, Wickham and Elizabeth find themselves in conversation, and she hears his story: he had planned on entering the ministry, rather than the militia, but was unable to do so because he lacked money. Darcy's father, Wickham says, had intended to provide for him, but Darcy used a loophole in the will to keep the money for himself.

Elizabeth, who instinctively likes and trusts Wickham, accepts his story immediately. Later in the evening, while she is watching Mr. Collins, Wickham tells her that Darcy is Lady Catherine de

Bourgh's nephew. He describes Lady Catherine as "dictatorial and insolent." Elizabeth leaves the party thinking of nothing "but Mr. Wickham, and what he had told her, all the way home." She decides that Darcy deserves nothing but contempt.

Elizabeth expresses these feelings to Jane the next day, and Jane defends Darcy, saying that there is probably a misunderstanding between the two men. Elizabeth will have none of it, and when Bingley invites the neighborhood to a ball the following Tuesday, she looks forward to seeing Wickham. Unfortunately, she is forced to promise the first two dances to Mr. Collins.

ANALYSIS: CHAPTERS 13–17

These chapters introduce Mr. Collins, the target of Jane Austen's greatest satire, and Wickham, the novel's most villainous character. Collins, a parody of a serious cleric, serves as a vehicle for criticism of the practice of entailment, by which the law forces Mr. Bennet to leave his property to such a ridiculous man instead of his own daughters. Collins functions as another example of Austen's criticism of snobbery. He differs, however, from Miss Bingley and Lady de Bourgh in that he is not snobbish because of his own rank; rather, he is snobbish by association. He is a man who believes wholeheartedly in class, even though he gains only the second helpings of its benefits. And in order to receive those benefits, he must toady himself to Lady de Bourgh. Rather than feel embarrassment at his behavior, he believes so strongly in the value conferred upon a person by class that he is full of self-importance because he has a noblewoman as his patroness.

Additionally, Collins's long, foolish speeches render him a prime example of Austen's talent for making stupidity comical. His absurdity increases as the story progresses, but even when the reader first meets him, he reveals himself to be so full of self-importance and exaggerated politeness that Mr. Bennet cannot resist making fun of him (Elizabeth's father suggests that Collins's pretense runs even deeper when he asks if his compliments are thought up in advance). With no sense of how foolish he sounds—none of the ridiculous characters in *Pride and Prejudice* are aware of their own absurdity—Mr. Collins replies that his flattering remarks "arise chiefly from what is passing at the time, and though I sometimes amuse myself with suggesting and arranging such elegant compliments as may be adapted to ordinary occasions, I always wish to give them as unstudied an air as possible." The reader can only agree with Mr. Bennet that "his cousin was as absurd" as he had hoped.

The arrival of Collins immediately precedes the first appearance of Wickham, and the clergyman's foolishness contrasts with Wickham's ability to charm. Wickham himself is one of the only male characters described by Austen as being extremely good-looking: his appeal exists only on the surface, but it is an attractive surface. This superficial appeal is crucial because it makes his story about Darcy's mistreatment of him believable, at least to Elizabeth. Darcy's pride has been obvious from his first appearance in the novel, but Elizabeth's decision to trust Wickham introduces her "prejudice" into the story. The reader may wonder about a man who tells self-pitying stories about his own life to a woman he barely knows, but Elizabeth seems to have few doubts—a testament, again, to the power of "first impressions" that is so important in the novel. She dislikes Darcy the first time she meets him. In contrast, she likes Wickham at their first acquaintance, leading her to believe his story even without hearing Darcy's side of it, and against Jane's greater sensibility.

These chapters also bring the reader to Mrs. Phillips's house for the first time. Mrs. Phillips is less shrill than her sister, Mrs. Bennet, but remains another low-class connection for the Bennet sisters to live down. Mr. Phillips is a Meryton attorney, which places him in a significantly lower station than the Darcys and Bingleys of the world.

CHAPTERS 18–23

SUMMARY: CHAPTER 18

Much to Elizabeth's dismay, Wickham does not attend the ball. Mr. Denny tells Elizabeth and Lydia that Darcy's presence keeps Wickham away from Netherfield. Elizabeth's unhappiness increases during two clumsy dances with Mr. Collins and reaches its peak when she finds herself dancing with Darcy. Their conversation is awkward, especially when she mentions Wickham, a subject Darcy clearly wishes to avoid. At the end of the dance, Elizabeth encounters Miss Bingley, who warns her not to trust Wickham. Elizabeth assumes that Bingley's sister is only being spiteful, however, and chooses to ignore the warning. Jane then tells her sister that she has asked Bingley for information about Wickham. But everything

Bingley knows about the officer comes from Darcy and is therefore (in Elizabeth's mind) suspect.

Mr. Collins, meanwhile, realizes that Darcy is related to his patroness, Lady Catherine. In spite of Elizabeth's best attempts to dissuade him, he introduces himself. Darcy treats Mr. Collins with contempt, but Mr. Collins is so obtuse that he does not notice.

At supper, Mrs. Bennet discusses the hoped-for union of Bingley and Jane so loudly that Elizabeth criticizes her, noting that Darcy is listening. Mrs. Bennet, however, ignores Elizabeth and continues rambling about the impending marriage. At the end of the meal, Mary performs a terrible song for the company, and Mr. Collins delivers a speech of epic and absurd pomposity. Elizabeth feels that her family has completely embarrassed itself.

SUMMARY: CHAPTERS 19–21

The next day, Mr. Collins proposes marriage to Elizabeth, assuming that she will be overjoyed. She turns him down as gently as possible, but he insists that she will change her mind shortly. Mrs. Bennet, who regards a match between her daughter and Mr. Collins as advantageous, is infuriated. She tells Elizabeth that if she does not marry Mr. Collins she will never see her again, and she asks Mr. Bennet to order Elizabeth to marry the clergyman. Her husband refuses and, befitting his wit and his desire to annoy his wife, actually informs his daughter that if she were to marry Mr. Collins, he would refuse to see her again.

A few days after the refused proposal, Elizabeth encounters Wickham in Meryton. He apologizes for his absence from the ball and walks her home, where Elizabeth introduces him to her parents. That same day, a letter arrives for Jane from Miss Bingley, informing her that Bingley and his party are returning to the city indefinitely and implying that Bingley plans to marry Darcy's sister, Georgiana. Elizabeth comforts Jane, telling her that this turn of events is all Miss Bingley's doing, not her brother's, and that Bingley will return to Netherfield.

SUMMARY: CHAPTERS 22–23

Suddenly, news arrives that Mr. Collins has proposed to Charlotte Lucas and that Elizabeth's friend has accepted. Elizabeth is shocked, despite Charlotte's insistence that the match is the best for which she could hope. Mrs. Bennet, of course, is furious with her daughter for allowing a husband to escape her, and as the days go by with no word from Bingley, Jane's marriage prospects, too, begin to appear limited.

Analysis: Chapters 18–23

Elizabeth's prejudice against Darcy survives these chapters, despite Miss Bingley's warning. It is difficult to blame Elizabeth for not seeing the truth, however. Austen has established Miss Bingley as a spiteful, treacherous figure in the preceding chapters, and Elizabeth has no reason to value her warning about Wickham more than the trust she instinctively places in him. Elizabeth's failure to ask Darcy about the matter directly while they are dancing is less excusable, however: she brings the issue up in a manner that assumes Wickham to be telling the truth (an assumption that is her key error). Unsurprisingly, Darcy is unwilling to talk given those terms.

The absurdity of Collins's snobbery is played to the hilt when he approaches Darcy and fails to notice the contempt with which Darcy replies to his introduction. Disdain and rejection do not have a place in Mr. Collins's perception of himself, by which his connection to Lady Catherine guarantees him a lofty place in society. His behavior in proposing to Elizabeth further illustrates his obtuseness. Austen tends to describe proposals in full only when they meet with rejection, primarily because rejections have so many comic and dramatic possibilities. Elizabeth's later rebuff of Darcy constitutes a thrilling moment in the story; here, Mr. Collins's lengthy speech is an opportunity for Austen to make him completely ridiculous. His refusal to accept "no" as an answer is, of course, unsurprising. His complete self-absorption blinds him to any answer other than "yes."

Mr. Collins's subsequent proposal to Charlotte Lucas, on the other hand, is far from comic because Charlotte accepts. Readers often argue that *Pride and Prejudice* and the rest of Austen's novels are unrealistic in their frequent portrayals of happy marriages. Charlotte's marriage to Collins injects a grim note into the romantic happiness that Elizabeth will later find. Indeed, one can interpret Charlotte's fate as a component of Austen's critique of a male-dominated society that leaves unmarried women without a future. Whereas Elizabeth is an idealist who will not marry solely for money, to either a fool (Collins) or a man she dislikes (Darcy, at first), Charlotte, six years older than her friend and lacking a fortune, is a pragmatist: she must capitalize on any opportunity that presents itself in order to avoid the societal scorn that accompanies old maid status. As Austen says of Charlotte: she "accepted [Mr. Collins] solely from the pure and disinterested desire of an establishment."

While the novel ultimately delivers Jane and Elizabeth to happiness, at this point in the story it seems as though the Bennet girls are losing out in their respective pursuits of husbands. When Charlotte says, "I am not a romantic you know . . . I ask only a comfortable home," it seems as though romanticism compels Elizabeth to ask for too much, to seek more than her society is willing to grant her.

Jane must now cope with the snobbery of Miss Bingley, who is apparently not content to disparage the Bennets solely orally, just as Elizabeth earlier faced Miss Bingley's scorn in reaction to Darcy's attraction to her. The suggestion in her letters that Bingley may marry Darcy's sister makes it clear that Miss Bingley, like Darcy himself, considers Jane too "low" to marry her brother. Indeed, while Darcy is later blamed for the temporary separation of Bingley and Jane, Miss Bingley's words and behavior suggest that she, too, plays a role in it.

CHAPTERS 24–26

SUMMARY: CHAPTERS 24–25

> *"My feelings will not be repressed. You must allow me to tell you how ardently I admire and love you."*
>
> *(See QUOTATIONS, p. 53)*

Miss Bingley sends another letter, this one praising the beauty and charm of Darcy's sister. The letter further states that Bingley will remain in London all winter, putting an end to the Bennets's hopes that he might return to Netherfield. Elizabeth is very upset by this news and complains to Jane that people lack "merit or sense," referring to Bingley for apparently abandoning Jane, and to Charlotte Lucas for agreeing to marry Mr. Collins. Meanwhile, Mrs. Bennet's hopes of seeing her daughters wed fade rapidly. Mr. Bennet seems amused: he encourages Elizabeth's interest in Wickham, so that she, like her sister, can be "crossed in love."

Mrs. Bennet's brother, Mr. Gardiner, comes to stay with the family. Immediately recognizing Jane's sadness, the Gardiners invite Jane to accompany them back to London when they finish their visit, hoping that a change in scenery might raise Jane's spirits. Jane accepts, excited also that in London she might get an opportunity to see Mr. Bingley. In the course of evenings spent with various friends and the military officers, Mrs. Gardiner notices that Elizabeth and Wickham, though not in any serious sort of love, show a definite preference for each other. Because of his lack of money, Mrs. Gardiner does not think of Wickham as a good match for Elizabeth, though she is fond of Wickham's stories of his life around Darcy's estate at Pemberley, which is near where Mrs. Gardiner grew up.

SUMMARY: CHAPTER 26

At the first opportunity, Mrs. Gardiner warns Elizabeth that Wickham's lack of money makes him an unsuitable match. She further says that Elizabeth should be careful not to embarrass her father by becoming attached to Wickham. Elizabeth responds carefully, stating that she will try to keep Wickham from falling in love with her and that she devoutly wishes not to upset her father, but concluding that all she can do is her best.

After Jane and the Gardiners depart for London, Mr. Collins returns from a visit to his parish for his wedding. Elizabeth reluctantly promises to visit Charlotte after her marriage. Meanwhile, Jane's letters from London recount how she called on Miss Bingley and how Miss Bingley was cold to her and visited her only briefly in return. Jane believes that Bingley's sister views her as an obstacle to her brother's marrying Georgiana Darcy.

Mrs. Gardiner writes to Elizabeth to ask about Wickham, and Elizabeth replies that his attentions have shifted to another girl, a Miss King, who has just inherited a large fortune. This turn of events touches Elizabeth's heart "but slightly . . . and her vanity was satisfied with believing that she would have been his only choice, had fortune permitted it." The narrator then goes on to point out that Elizabeth's equanimity about Wickham trying to marry for money is somewhat out of joint with her disgust that Charlotte would do the same thing. As for Elizabeth, the very limited pain that Wickham's transfer of affections causes her makes her believe she was never in love with him.

ANALYSIS: CHAPTERS 24–26

The first three chapters of Book Two introduce the Gardiners, who prove to be Elizabeth's most sensible relatives. They often seem to act as surrogate parents to Jane and Elizabeth. The nurturing and supportive Gardiners take Jane to London to distract her from her unhappiness over Bingley. However amusing the reader finds him, Mr. Bennet, in contrast, seems to have no real understanding of

SUMMARY & ANALYSIS

when his children even need help. He prefers withdrawing into the peace of his library to coping with the problems facing his family. In particular, Mr. Bennet's amusement at his wife's distress and his suggestion that Elizabeth develop a crush on Wickham emphasize the extent to which he has abandoned the paternal role in the family. His wit and intelligence make him a sympathetic character in many ways, but he seems to absent himself from important matters. Later in the novel, his negligence allows Lydia to go to Brighton for the summer and then to elope with Wickham. At this point in the novel, Austen compels her reader to contrast Mr. Bennet's unhelpful suggestion about Wickham with Mrs. Gardiner's recognition that the officer is not a suitable match for her niece.

Mrs. Gardiner's observation about Wickham raises an interesting irony. Wickham is not suitable for Elizabeth for the same reason Elizabeth is not suitable for Darcy. Elizabeth's response to Mrs. Gardiner's warning is equivocal, suggesting first that she recognizes this irony but also that she is aware that, though social strictures on marriage might be illogical and unromantic, were she to break them she would be negatively affecting her family. Elizabeth and Austen are both saved from having to worry about this moral conundrum when Wickham shifts his affections to the suddenly wealthy Miss King. The narrator's comment that Elizabeth's feelings about Wickham's decision to marry for money do not match her feelings about Charlotte's similar decision imply that there is a double standard at work in Elizabeth's logic: though she seems to consider it acceptable for men to marry for money, she believes so strongly in love that she believes her female friends should ignore such considerations.

While Elizabeth may forgive Wickham for chasing Ms. King's money, the reader is more likely to see him as a simple fortune hunter. By establishing this aspect of his character, Austen prepares the reader for the revelation that Wickham attempted to elope with Darcy's sister in order to obtain her fortune. In this seemingly minor fact, which Elizabeth herself seems to brush aside, resides a clue to Wickham's generally poor character.

CHAPTERS 27–34

SUMMARY: CHAPTERS 27–29
In March, Elizabeth travels with Sir William Lucas to visit Charlotte and her new husband, Mr. Collins. On the way, they spend a night

in London with Jane and the Gardiners. Elizabeth and Mrs. Gardiner speak about Wickham's attempts to win over Miss King. Mrs. Gardiner is critical of him, calling him a "mercenary," but Elizabeth defends him, calling him prudent. Before Elizabeth leaves London, the Gardiners invite her to accompany them on a tour, perhaps out to the lakes. Elizabeth gleefully accepts.

When Elizabeth arrives in Hunsford, the location of Mr. Collins's parish, the clergyman greets her enthusiastically, as does Charlotte. On the second day of her visit, she sees Miss de Bourgh, Lady de Bourgh's daughter, from a window. The girl is "sickly and cross," Elizabeth decides, and she imagines with some satisfaction Darcy's marrying such an unappealing person. Miss de Bourgh invites them to dine at Rosings, a mansion that awes even Sir William Lucas with its grandeur.

At dinner, Lady Catherine dominates the conversation. After the meal, she grills Elizabeth concerning her upbringing, deciding that the Bennet sisters have been badly reared. The failure of Mrs. Bennet to hire a governess, the girls' lack of musical and artistic talents, and Elizabeth's own impudence are all mentioned before the end of the evening.

SUMMARY: CHAPTERS 30–32

Sir William departs after a week, satisfied with his daughter's contentment. Shortly thereafter, Darcy and a cousin named Colonel Fitzwilliam visit their aunt at Rosings. When Mr. Collins pays his respects, the two men accompany him back to his parsonage and visit briefly with Elizabeth and Charlotte.

Another invitation to Rosings follows, and Colonel Fitzwilliam pays special attention to Elizabeth during the dinner. After the meal, she plays the pianoforte and pokes fun at Darcy, informing Colonel Fitzwilliam of his bad behavior at the Meryton ball, at which he refused to dance with her. Lady Catherine lectures Elizabeth on the proper manner of playing the instrument, forcing Elizabeth to remain at the keyboard until the end of the evening.

The next day, Darcy visits the parsonage and tells Elizabeth that Bingley is unlikely to spend much of his time at Netherfield Park in the future. The rest of their conversation is awkward, and when Darcy departs, Charlotte declares that he must be in love with Elizabeth, or he would never have called in such an odd manner. In the days that follow, both Darcy and his cousin visit frequently, however, and eventually Charlotte surmises that it is perhaps Colonel Fitzwilliam who is interested in Elizabeth.

SUMMARY: CHAPTERS 33–34

Elizabeth encounters Darcy and his cousin frequently in her walks through the countryside. During one conversation, Colonel Fitzwilliam mentions that Darcy claims to have recently saved a friend from an imprudent marriage. Elizabeth conjectures that the "friend" was Bingley and the "imprudent marriage" a marriage to Jane. She views Darcy as the agent of her sister's unhappiness.

Alone at the parsonage, Elizabeth is still mulling over what Fitzwilliam has told her when Darcy enters and abruptly declares his love for her. His proposal of marriage dwells at length upon her social inferiority, and Elizabeth's initially polite rejection turns into an angry accusation. She demands to know if he sabotaged Jane's romance with Bingley; he admits that he did. She then repeats Wickham's accusations and declares that she thinks Darcy to be proud and selfish and that marriage to him is utterly unthinkable. Darcy grimly departs.

ANALYSIS: CHAPTERS 27–34

Mrs. Gardiner tends to function as the voice of reason in the novel, and her criticism of Wickham counters Elizabeth's unwillingness to question his purposes. Mrs. Gardiner ascribes a mercenary motive to Wickham's interest in Miss King, whereas Elizabeth defends him by asking her aunt "what . . . the difference [is] in matrimonial affairs, between the mercenary and the prudent motive." This does seem a fine question, and not one her aunt can readily answer. But in asking the question, Elizabeth seems to violate her own principles—she herself has already refused to marry Mr. Collins for social advantage, and she does so again when Darcy proposes. It appears that sympathy for Wickham leads Elizabeth to betray her conscience.

The visit to Rosings introduces Lady Catherine de Bourgh, who serves as another vehicle for Austen's criticism of snobbery. Lady Catherine's favorite pastime is ordering everyone else about ("Elizabeth found that nothing was beneath this great Lady's attention, which could furnish her with an occasion of dictating to others"). The only individual who dares to stand up to the haughty Lady Catherine is Elizabeth (unsurprisingly, as elsewhere she sees through the pretensions of pompous and arrogant people like Mr. Collins and

Miss Bingley). When Lady Catherine criticizes the Bennet sisters' upbringing, Elizabeth defends her family, "suspect[ing] herself to be the first creature who had ever dared to trifle with so much dignified impertinence." The same dignified impertinence with which Elizabeth combats Lady Catherine's preconceptions reappears later in her refusal to let Lady Catherine prevent her from marrying Darcy.

Darcy's proposal is the turning point of *Pride and Prejudice*. Until he asks her to marry him, Elizabeth's main preoccupation with Darcy centers around dislike; after the proposal, the novel chronicles the slow, steady growth of her love. At the moment, however, Elizabeth's attitude toward Darcy corresponds to the judgments she has already made about him. She refuses him because she thinks that he is too arrogant, part of her first impression of him at the Meryton ball, and because of the role she believes he played in disinheriting Wickham and his admitted role in disrupting the romance between Jane and Bingley.

Just as Elizabeth yields to her prejudices (she has not yet heard Darcy's side of the story), Darcy allows his pride to guide him. In his proposal to Elizabeth, he spends more time emphasizing Elizabeth's lower rank than actually asking her to marry him ("he was not more eloquent on the subject of tenderness than of pride"). This turning point thus occurs with the two central characters occupying seemingly irreconcilable emotional locations, leaving the reader, in the words of critic Douglas Bush, "almost exactly in the middle of the book, wondering if and how the chasm . . . can be bridged."

CHAPTERS 35–42

SUMMARY: CHAPTERS 35–36

The following day, Elizabeth takes a walk and runs into Darcy, who gives her a letter. He walks away, and Elizabeth begins to read it. In the letter, Darcy again admits to attempting to break Bingley's romance with Jane, but he defends himself by arguing that Jane's attachment to his friend was not yet strong enough to lead to heartbreak. He adds that he did not wish Bingley to involve himself with the social encumbrance of marrying into the Bennet family, with its lack of both wealth and propriety. In relation to Wickham, the letter states that Darcy did provide for him after his father's death and that the root of their quarrel lay in an attempt by Wickham to elope with Darcy's sister, Georgiana, in the hopes of obtaining her fortune.

Elizabeth is stunned by this revelation, and while she dismisses some of what Darcy says about Jane and Bingley, his account of Wickham's doings causes her to reappraise the officer and decide that she was probably wrong to trust him. Her feelings toward Darcy suddenly enter into flux.

SUMMARY: CHAPTERS 37–39

Darcy and Colonel Fitzwilliam leave Rosings. A week later, Elizabeth departs the parsonage, despite Lady Catherine's insistence that she stay another two weeks. Before Elizabeth leaves, Mr. Collins informs her that he and Charlotte seem to be made for one another (which is clearly not true). He wishes Elizabeth the same happiness in marriage that he himself enjoys.

After a short stay at the Gardiners's London house, Elizabeth, joined by Jane, returns home. The two are met by Catherine and Lydia, who talk of nothing but the soldiers as they ride home in their father's coach. The regiment is to be sent to Brighton for the summer, and the two girls are hoping to convince their parents to summer there also. In the course of the conversation, Lydia mentions, with some satisfaction, that Wickham is no longer interested in Miss King, who has gone to Liverpool to stay with her uncle.

Mr. and Mrs. Bennet welcome their daughters home, and the Lucases come for dinner. Lydia prattles about the exciting coach ride and insists that the girls go to Meryton to see the officers. Not wanting to see Wickham, Elizabeth refuses.

SUMMARY: CHAPTERS 40–42

Elizabeth tells Jane the truth about Wickham. They debate whether to expose him publicly, ultimately deciding against it. Meanwhile, Mrs. Bennet continues to bemoan the loss of Mr. Bingley as a husband for Jane and voices her displeasure at the happy marriage of Charlotte and Mr. Collins. Lydia is invited to spend the summer in Brighton by the wife of a Colonel Forster. Mr. Bennet allows her to go, assuming that the colonel will keep her out of trouble.

Elizabeth sees Wickham once more before his regiment departs, and they discuss Darcy in a guarded manner. Elizabeth avoids any mention of what she has discovered. The soldiers leave Meryton for Brighton; Kitty is distraught to see them go and even more distraught that her sister is allowed to follow them.

In July, Elizabeth accompanies the Gardiners on a tour of the Derbyshire countryside, and their travels take them close to Darcy's manor, Pemberley. Hearing that Darcy is not in the neighborhood, she agrees to take a tour of the estate.

_____

ANALYSIS: CHAPTERS 35–42

Darcy's letter begins a humbling process for both Elizabeth and him, which results in a maturation of each of their attitudes toward the other. In Darcy's case, the rejection of his proposal strikes a blow to his pride and compels him to respond to Elizabeth's anger. The resulting letter reveals to Elizabeth how she misjudged both him and Wickham. With the extent of her mistaken prejudice suddenly apparent, she is humbled enough to begin to look at Darcy in a new light.

Some critics maintain that Darcy's letter is unrealistic, contending that such a proud and reserved man would never reveal so many details of his private life. In this view, the letter functions primarily as an artificial device through which Austen is able to introduce a large quantity of information while vindicating Darcy. One can argue, however, that the "dreadful bitterness of spirit" in which Darcy claims to have written the letter explains its uncharacteristic nature. Regardless of its realism, the letter serves its purpose: it reveals the truth about Wickham's relationship to Darcy and consequently shifts sympathy from Wickham to Darcy. It is interesting to note that the idea of a man eloping with a young woman was clichéd in the literature of Austen's era; nevertheless, its appearance in *Pride and Prejudice* serves a vital function, as it later provides Darcy with a motive (besides his love of Elizabeth) for helping Lydia after she elopes with Wickham.

After the reception of the letter, the novel contrives to separate Darcy and Elizabeth, giving each of them space in which to adjust their feelings and behavior. In the meantime, Austen lays the groundwork for Lydia's whirlwind romance with Wickham and establishes a contrast between Elizabeth's maturity concerning Darcy and Lydia's girlish imprudence. Whereas Elizabeth assumes a passive stance in matters of love, consenting to go to Pemberley only because she thinks Darcy will not be there, Lydia actively pursues her beloved officers and stakes her claim to Wickham now that he has lost interest in Miss King: "I will answer for it that he never cared three straws for her."

That Mr. Bennet is unaware of Lydia's infatuation with the officer and permits her to follow the militia to Brighton reminds us of his irresponsible detachment from family life. Because of their decision not to expose Wickham, Jane and Elizabeth are also partly responsible for Lydia's imminent romance. Darcy maintains a similar silence about Wickham's past, which brings him into the beginnings of an alignment with Elizabeth.

CHAPTERS 43–45

SUMMARY: CHAPTER 43

> *. . . and at that moment she felt that to be mistress of Pemberley might be something!*
>
> *(See* QUOTATIONS, *p. 54)*

As Elizabeth tours the beautiful estate of Pemberley with the Gardiners, she imagines what it would be like to be mistress there, as Darcy's wife. The housekeeper, Mrs. Reynolds, shows them portraits of Darcy and Wickham and relates that Darcy, in his youth, was "the sweetest, most generous-hearted boy in the world." She adds that he is the kindest of masters: "I have never had a cross word from him in my life." Elizabeth is surprised to hear such an agreeable description of a man she considers unbearably arrogant.

While Elizabeth and the Gardiners continue to explore the grounds, Darcy himself suddenly appears. He joins them in their walk, proving remarkably polite. Elizabeth is immediately embarrassed at having come to Pemberley after the events of recent months, and she assures Darcy that she came only because she thought that he was away. Darcy tells her that he has just arrived to prepare his home for a group of guests that includes the Bingleys and his own sister, Georgiana. He asks Elizabeth if she would like to meet Georgiana, and Elizabeth replies that she would. After Darcy leaves them, the Gardiners comment on his good looks and good manners, so strikingly divergent from the account of Darcy's character that Elizabeth has given them.

SUMMARY: CHAPTERS 44–45

The next day, Darcy and Georgiana, who is pretty but very shy, visit Elizabeth at her inn. Bingley joins them, and after a brief visit, they invite Elizabeth and the Gardiners, who perceive that Darcy is in love with their niece, to dine at Pemberley. The following morning, Elizabeth and Mrs. Gardiner visit Pemberley to call on Miss Darcy. Bingley's sisters are both present; when Darcy enters the room, Miss Bingley makes a spiteful comment to Elizabeth, noting that the departure of the militia from Meryton "must be a great loss to your family." Elizabeth dodges the subject of Wickham. This deflection proves fortunate given the presence of Georgiana, as references to the man with whom she almost eloped would embarrass her.

After the guests depart, Miss Bingley attempts to criticize Elizabeth to Darcy, and makes a light remark about how he once thought Elizabeth "rather pretty." Darcy replies that he now considers Elizabeth "one of the handsomest women of my acquaintance."

ANALYSIS: CHAPTERS 43–45

Elizabeth's visit to Pemberley constitutes a critical step in her progress toward marrying Darcy. The house itself is representative, even a symbol, of its owner—the narrator describes it as a "large, handsome, stone building, standing well on rising ground . . . in front, a stream of some natural importance was swelled into greater, but without any artificial appearance. Its banks were neither formal, nor falsely adorned." Darcy is similarly large and handsome, elevated socially just as his house is elevated physically. The description of the way the stream's "natural importance was swelled into greater" reminds the reader of Darcy's pride; that the stream is "neither formal, nor falsely adorned," however, reminds the reader of Darcy's honesty and lack of pretense. Most importantly, the property delights Elizabeth, foreshadowing her eventual realization that the master of Pemberley similarly delights her.

Mrs. Reynolds's glowing descriptions of Darcy continue the process of breaking down Elizabeth's initial prejudice against him. As Mrs. Reynolds reveals a hidden side of Darcy, Elizabeth realizes how hastily she has judged him. This ability to admit the error of her ways demonstrates Elizabeth's emotional maturity; unlike Miss Bingley, who resorts to denigrating Elizabeth when she realizes that Darcy favors her, Elizabeth does not allow arrogance to prevent her from confronting her own shortcomings.

The arrival of Darcy himself further encourages Elizabeth's change of heart. Humbled by her rejection of his marriage proposal, Darcy has altered his conduct toward her and become a perfect gentleman. This courteous behavior both illustrates his love for her and compels the growth of her estimation of him. His ability to overcome his pride in much the same way that Elizabeth overcomes her prejudice gives Elizabeth and the reader hope that her rejection of him has not caused him to give up and that he may propose again under different terms.

The reader meets Georgiana Darcy for the first time in these chapters. Previously, she has been described as a possible wife for Mr. Bingley because of her beauty and accomplishments. In person, however, she is painfully shy; as a result, the reader ceases to see her as a threat to Jane. She cuts a very different figure—and one with whom the reader can sympathize—from the overeager Miss Bingley, whose aggressive pursuit of Darcy highlights her obnoxiousness. Indeed, Miss Bingley reappears with more spite than before. The mean-spiritedness behind her derisive insinuation about the Bennet girls' unladylike obsession with the soldiers contrasts with Elizabeth's thoughtful protection of the vulnerable Georgiana.

CHAPTERS 46–49

SUMMARY: CHAPTER 46

When Elizabeth returns to her inn, she finds two letters from Jane: the first relates that Lydia has eloped with Wickham, the second that there is no word from the couple and that they may not be married yet. Elizabeth panics, realizing that if Wickham does not marry Lydia, the reputations of both Lydia and the entire family will be ruined.

As Elizabeth rushes out to find the Gardiners, Darcy appears and she tells him the story. Darcy immediately blames himself for not exposing Wickham, and Elizabeth blames herself for the same reason. She decides to return home immediately. After an apology to Darcy and his sister for breaking their dinner engagement, Elizabeth and the Gardiners hasten back to the Bennet home in Longbourn.

SUMMARY: CHAPTER 47

On the way home, Mr. Gardiner attempts to reassure his niece that Wickham will certainly marry Lydia because he will not want his own career and reputation ruined. Elizabeth replies by telling them generally about Wickham's past behavior, without revealing the details of his romance with Darcy's sister. When she gets home, Elizabeth learns that her father has gone to London in search of Lydia and Wickham. Mrs. Bennet, of course, is hysterical, blaming Colonel Forster for not taking care of her daughter. In private, Jane assures Elizabeth that there was no way anyone could have known about their sister's attachment to Wickham. Fretfully, they examine the letter that Lydia left for Colonel Forster's wife, in which she looks forward to signing her name "Lydia Wickham."

SUMMARY: CHAPTER 48

Mr. Gardiner follows Mr. Bennet to London and writes to Long-bourn a few days later with the news that the search has been un-successful so far. He reports that Mr. Bennet is now going to every hotel in turn looking for the couple. Meanwhile, a letter arrives from Mr. Collins that, in his usual manner, accuses the Bennets of poor parenting and notes that Lydia's behavior reflects poorly on the family as a whole. More time passes before Mr. Gardiner writes to say that attempts to trace Wickham through friends and family have failed. The letter further says, to Mrs. Bennet's consternation, that Mr. Bennet is returning home.

SUMMARY: CHAPTER 49

Two days after Mr. Bennet returns to Longbourn, Mr. Gardiner writes to tell him that Wickham and Lydia have been found and that Wickham will marry her if the Bennets will guarantee him a small income. Mr. Bennet gladly acquiesces, deciding that marriage to a scoundrel is better than a ruined reputation.

The Bennets assume that the Gardiners have paid Wickham a sizable amount to get him to agree to the wedding. Not "a farthing less than ten thousand pounds," Mr. Bennet guesses. The Bennets assume that they owe a deep debt to their relatives. Mrs. Bennet is deliriously happy at having Lydia married, even when her husband and daughters point out how much it has probably cost. Her happiness is tempered when her husband refuses to allow Wickham and Lydia to visit or to provide his newly married daughter with money to purchase clothes.

ANALYSIS: CHAPTERS 46–49

The plot, which had slowed since Darcy's proposal, now picks up speed as it rushes toward its conclusion. Amid the turmoil of Lydia's folly, Elizabeth turns immediately to Darcy, illustrating the close-ness developing between them. Their shared sense of guilt about failing to expose Wickham's true nature (which they believe would have prevented the elopement) aligns them emotionally and gives them a common purpose.

Though she and her husband are obviously at fault, Mrs. Bennet reacts to the news of Lydia's elopement by blaming Colonel Forster. The Bennet parents come across as highly inadequate at this point in the text—Mrs. Bennet because of her stupidity and Mr. Bennet because of his refusal to take responsibility for his children. The issue for Jane and Elizabeth about family connections has receded somewhat into the background, but here it reappears and reminds the reader that the Bennet parents' lack of refinement still threatens the prospective romances of the two eldest Bennet daughters.

During the crisis, the Gardiners again step forward to act responsibly. It is Mr. Gardiner, rather than Mr. Bennet, who takes charge of the search in the city—Mr. Bennet even returns home after a time. (Mrs. Bennet's fear that her husband will die in London and leave her destitute typifies her general tendency to ignore real problems and magnify trivial ones.) It is not terribly surprising that Mr. Gardiner apparently finds Lydia, or even that he apparently pays Wickham to convince him to marry her. He is simply filling the adult role that the Bennet parents have vacated.

Pride and Prejudice is critical of the difficulties faced by women in English society of the period. Whereas Austen passes judgment on both the practice of entailment and the necessity of marriage for women to avoid public scorn (which leads to Charlotte's union with Mr. Collins for practicality's sake), she does not question the idea that living with a man out of wedlock ruins a girl. Elizabeth, the voice of reason and common sense at this point in the novel, condemns Lydia's behavior as "infamy" and declares that if Lydia does not marry Wickham, "she is lost forever." The only voice of moral relativism belongs to Mrs. Bennet, who is so happy to have Lydia married that she does not care about the manner of the marriage's accomplishment. While Lydia may have escaped social stigma, Mr. Bennet still condemns her and Wickham, saying, "I will not encourage the impudence of either, by receiving them at Longbourn." Though she criticizes sexism, Austen lets bourgeois morality alone.

CHAPTERS 50–55

SUMMARY: CHAPTERS 50–51

Elizabeth realizes that her opinion of Darcy has changed so completely that if he were to propose to her again, she would accept. She understands, however, that, given Lydia's embarrassing behavior and the addition of Wickham to the Bennet family, such a proposal seems extremely unlikely.

Mr. Gardiner writes to Mr. Bennet again to inform him that Wickham has accepted a commission in the North of England. Lydia asks to be allowed to visit her family before she goes north with her new husband. After much disagreement, the Bennets allow the

newlyweds to stay at their home. The ten-day visit is difficult: Lydia is oblivious to all of the trouble that she has caused, and Wickham behaves as if he has done nothing wrong. One morning while sitting with Jane and Elizabeth, Lydia describes her wedding and mentions that Darcy was in the church. Elizabeth is amazed and sends a letter to Mrs. Gardiner asking for details.

SUMMARY: CHAPTERS 52–53

Mrs. Gardiner replies to Elizabeth that it was Darcy who found Lydia and Wickham, and Darcy who paid Wickham the money that facilitated the marriage. She drops hints that Darcy did so because of his love for Elizabeth. Elizabeth's surprise is immense, and she is unsure whether to be upset or pleased.

After Wickham and Lydia depart for their new home in the North, news arrives that Bingley is returning to Netherfield Park for a few weeks. Mr. Bennet refuses to visit him, much to the family's discomfort. Three days after his arrival at Netherfield, however, Bingley comes to the Bennets's home, accompanied by Darcy. Mrs. Bennet is overly attentive to Bingley and quite rude to Darcy, completely unaware that he was the one who saved Lydia. Before departing, the gentlemen promise to dine at Longbourn soon.

SUMMARY: CHAPTERS 54–55

Darcy and Bingley come to dinner; Bingley places himself next to Jane and pays her much attention while Darcy finds a seat at the opposite end of the table from Elizabeth, rendering conversation between the two impossible. Elizabeth accepts that having been refused by her once, Darcy will not ask her to marry him again.

Bingley visits the Bennets a few days later, and Mrs. Bennet invites him to dinner. He tells her that he is already engaged for the day but eagerly accepts an invitation for the following day. He calls so early in the morning that he arrives before the women have gotten dressed. After the meal, Mrs. Bennet manages (clumsily) to leave Bingley alone with Jane but he does not propose. The following day, however, Bingley goes shooting with Mr. Bennet and stays for dinner. After the meal, he finds himself alone with Jane again. This time, he tells her that he will ask Mr. Bennet for permission to marry her. Mr. Bennet happily agrees and Jane tells Elizabeth that she is "the happiest creature in the world."

The engagement settled, Bingley comes to visit often. Jane learns that he had no idea that she was in London over the winter, and she realizes that his sisters were attempting to keep him away from her. Meanwhile, the neighborhood agrees that the Bennets are extremely fortunate in their daughter's marriage.

ANALYSIS: CHAPTERS 50–55

Elizabeth's realization that Darcy is "exactly the man, who, in disposition and talents, would most suit her" is ironic, since she not only rejected his marriage proposal earlier but did so in a manner that made it clear that she despised him. To Elizabeth, the irony is obvious: "she became jealous of his esteem, when she could no longer hope to be benefited by it . . . she wanted to hear of him, when there seemed the least chance of gaining intelligence." Her feelings toward Darcy are now what his were toward her earlier; she assumes that he has changed his mind and that her change of heart has come too late. For even if Darcy were still interested in her, Lydia's elopement seems likely to have destroyed any chance of his proposing again. The Lydia-Wickham affair serves as a reminder of Darcy's original objection to marrying Elizabeth, and Elizabeth believes that he must certainly consider it a symptom of the poor breeding of her family and an example of the embarrassment that association with her family would bring him.

While Elizabeth's hope of Darcy's still loving her slowly grows in these chapters, the reader receives hints all along that Darcy's feelings for her have not altered. He has paid for Lydia's wedding, and the insightful Mrs. Gardiner, who provides levelheaded analyses of situations at various points in the novel, can think of only one reason for him to do so. Elizabeth's instincts tell her the same thing: "Her heart did whisper, that he had done it for her." Nevertheless, she insists on squashing that whisper, as her embarrassment about Lydia and her sense of Darcy's pride compel her to the assumption that Darcy would never connect himself with her family, especially now that the odious Wickham is her brother-in-law.

The happy conclusion to Bingley's courtship of Jane suggests that Darcy no longer cares about the Bennet sisters' low social status. As evidence that Darcy has overcome this important obstacle at least to some, he now does nothing to dissuade his friend from tying himself to a disreputable family. Whereas Darcy previously disrupted the romance between Bingley and Jane in order to protect his friend's social status, he now allows their love to triumph over their class difference, despite Lydia's elopement scandal, which he could easily have used as an excuse to distance himself and his friends from the Bennets. Austen does not allow Elizabeth to assume anything from

Jane's engagement, but the reader is allowed to assume that another wedding will follow.

CHAPTERS 56–61

SUMMARY: CHAPTER 56

A week after Bingley and Jane become engaged, Lady Catherine de Bourgh visits the Bennets. The noblewoman wants to speak with Elizabeth and insists that they walk outside to hold a conversation. There, Lady Catherine informs Elizabeth that she has heard a rumor that Darcy is planning to marry her. Such a notion, Lady Catherine insists, is ridiculous, given Elizabeth's low station in life and the tacit engagement of Darcy to her own daughter.

Elizabeth conceals her surprise at this news and acts very coolly toward Lady Catherine. She admits that she and Darcy are not engaged but, despite the noblewoman's demands, refuses to promise not to enter into an engagement to him. Lady Catherine claims that Elizabeth is bound to obey her by "the claims of duty, honour, and gratitude." She presents the familiar objection: the Bennets have such low connections that Darcy's marrying Elizabeth would "ruin him in the opinion of all his friends, and make him the contempt of the world." Elizabeth defends her family, declaring, "I am a gentleman's daughter," and then asserts her independence from the exasperating control that such snobs as Mr. Collins, Miss Bingley, and Lady Catherine herself always attempt to exert over their social inferiors. "I am . . . resolved," she says, "to act in that manner, which will, in my own opinion, constitute my happiness, without reference to you, or to any person so wholly unconnected with me." Lady Catherine leaves, furious and frustrated, and Elizabeth keeps their conversation secret.

SUMMARY: CHAPTERS 57–58

> "My affections and wishes are unchanged, but one
> word from you will silence me on this subject forever."
> (See QUOTATIONS, p. 55)

A short time later, a letter arrives from Mr. Collins that suggests that an engagement between Darcy and Elizabeth is imminent. The letter comes to Mr. Bennet, who reads it to Elizabeth and comments on the absurdity of the idea of an engagement with Darcy—"who never looked at any woman but to see a blemish, and who probably never looked at you in his life."

A little while after Lady Catherine's visit, Darcy again comes to stay with Bingley at Netherfield. The two friends visit the Bennets, and everyone takes a walk together. Elizabeth and Darcy lag behind, and when they are alone, Elizabeth thanks him for his generosity in saving Lydia's good name. Darcy replies that he did so only because Lydia is her sister. He then says that his feelings toward her have not changed since his proposal. Elizabeth tells him that her own feelings have changed and that she is now willing to marry him.

SUMMARY: CHAPTERS 59–60

That night, Elizabeth tells Jane about Darcy's intention to marry her. Jane, stunned, cannot believe that Elizabeth truly loves Darcy. Elizabeth promises Jane that she does. The next day, Darcy and Elizabeth walk together again, and that night Darcy goes to Mr. Bennet to ask him for his consent to the match.

Like Jane, Mr. Bennet needs Elizabeth to convince him that she does indeed care for Darcy. After she assures him of her love, she tells him how Darcy paid off Wickham. Mrs. Bennet then learns of her daughter's engagement and is actually struck dumb for a time before bursting into cries of delight.

Darcy and Elizabeth discuss how their love began and how it developed. Darcy writes to inform Lady Catherine of his engagement, while Mr. Bennet sends a letter to Mr. Collins to do likewise. The Collinses come to Longbourn to congratulate the couple (and escape an angry Lady Catherine), as do the Lucases and Mrs. Phillips.

SUMMARY: CHAPTER 61

After the weddings, Bingley purchases an estate near Pemberley, and the Bennet sisters visit one another frequently. Kitty is kept away from Lydia and her bad influence, and she matures greatly by spending time at her elder sisters' homes. Lydia and Wickham remain incorrigible, asking Darcy for money and visiting the Bingleys so frequently that even the good-humored Bingley grows tired of them. Elizabeth becomes great friends with Georgiana. She even comes to interact on decent terms with Miss Bingley. Lady Catherine eventually accepts the marriage and visits her nephew and his wife at Pemberley. Darcy and Elizabeth continue to consider the Gardiners close friends, grateful for the fact that they brought Elizabeth to Pemberley the first time and helped to bring the two together.

ANALYSIS: CHAPTERS 56–61

Lady Catherine is the last of the many obstacles facing the romance between Darcy and Elizabeth, and Elizabeth's confrontation with her marks the heroine's finest moment. This encounter crystallizes the tensions that their difference in social status has created. All of the qualities that Elizabeth has embodied thus far—intelligence, wit, lack of pretense, and resistance to snobbery—are evident in her dialogue. Lady Catherine, with the weight of birth and money on her side, responds to Elizabeth's brazenness with a snobbishness that reflects her unassailable preoccupation with social concerns and demonstrates her lack of appreciation for the richness of Elizabeth's character. Elizabeth, of course, has not yet received a new proposal of marriage from Darcy and has no way of knowing if one is forthcoming, but her pride in herself and her love of Darcy allow her to stand up to the domineering Lady Catherine. With the expression of her beliefs, Elizabeth demonstrates the enduring strength of her will and self-respect.

After the dynamic confrontation between these two firebrands, Darcy's proposal, theoretically the climax of the novel, is almost a letdown. As noted previously, Austen rarely stages successful proposals in full; accordingly, the narrator summarizes Elizabeth's affirmative response to Darcy's bid in a brief paragraph. Some critics argue that the novel becomes simplistic in this third and final part—that Darcy's character changes too drastically from the arrogant figure of the opening chapters. One can also argue, however, that his initial pride feeds to some extent off of Elizabeth's initial prejudice, and that as one dissolves as its bearer matures, so does the other.

It is the nature of Austen's novels that romance must win out over all of the obstacles, whether social or personal, that it faces. Just as love triumphs over pride in social status for Darcy, it triumphs over prejudice for Elizabeth. Elizabeth's friends and family, thinking that she dislikes Darcy, ask her if she is marrying for love; in the end, in Austen, despite the undeniably relevant social issues of class, money, and practicality, this question always proves most important.

IMPORTANT QUOTATIONS EXPLAINED

1.   It is a truth universally acknowledged, that a single man in possession of a good fortune, must be in want of a wife.

This is the first sentence of *Pride and Prejudice* and stands as one of the most famous first lines in literature. Even as it briskly introduces the arrival of Mr. Bingley at Netherfield—the event that sets the novel in motion—this sentence also offers a miniature sketch of the entire plot, which concerns itself with the pursuit of "single men in possession of a good fortune" by various female characters. The preoccupation with socially advantageous marriage in nineteenth-century English society manifests itself here, for in claiming that a single man "must be in want of a wife," the narrator reveals that the reverse is also true: a single woman, whose socially prescribed options are quite limited, is in (perhaps desperate) want of a husband.

2. "Which do you mean?" and turning round, he looked for a moment at Elizabeth, till catching her eye, he withdrew his own and coldly said, "She is tolerable; but not handsome enough to tempt me; and I am in no humour at present to give consequence to young ladies who are slighted by other men. You had better return to your partner and enjoy her smiles, for you are wasting your time with me."

These words describe Darcy's reaction at the Meryton ball in Chapter 3 to Bingley's suggestion that he dance with Elizabeth. Darcy, who sees the people of Meryton as his social inferiors, haughtily refuses to condescend to dancing with someone "not handsome enough" for him. Moreover, he does so within range of Elizabeth, thereby establishing a reputation among the entire community for pride and bad manners. His sense of social superiority, artfully exposed in this passing comment, later proves his chief difficulty in admitting his love for Elizabeth. The rudeness with which Darcy treats Elizabeth creates a negative impression of him in her mind, one that will linger for nearly half of the novel, until the underlying nobility of his character is gradually revealed to her.

QUOTATIONS

3. "In vain have I struggled. It will not do. My feelings will
    not be repressed. You must allow me to tell you how
    ardently I admire and love you." Elizabeth's astonishment
    was beyond expression. She stared, coloured, doubted, and
    was silent. This he considered sufficient encouragement,
    and the avowal of all that he felt and had long felt for
    her, immediately followed. He spoke well, but there were
    feelings besides those of the heart to be detailed, and
    he not more eloquent on the subject of tenderness
    than of pride. His sense of her inferiority—of its being
    a degradation—of the family obstacles which judgment
    had always opposed to inclination, were dwelt on with
    a warmth which seemed due to the consequence he was
    wounding, but was very unlikely to recommend his suit.

Darcy's proposal of marriage to Elizabeth in Chapter 34 demonstrates how his feelings toward her transformed since his earlier dismissal of her as "not handsome enough." While Elizabeth rejects his proposal, this event marks the turning point in the novel. Before Darcy asks Elizabeth to marry him, she feels only contempt for him; afterward, she begins to see him in a new light, as certain incidents help illustrate the essential goodness of his character. At this moment, however, Elizabeth's eventual change of heart remains unforeseen—all she thinks of is Darcy's arrogance, his attempts to interfere in Bingley's courtship of Jane, and his alleged mistreatment of Wickham. Her judgment of Darcy stems from her initial prejudice against his snobbishness, just as his pride about his high social status hampers his attempt to express his affection. As the above quote makes clear, he spends more time emphasizing her lower rank and unsuitability for marriage to him than he does complimenting her or pledging his love. "He was not more eloquent on the subject of tenderness than of pride," the narrator states; Darcy must prioritize love over his sense of superiority before he is worthy of Elizabeth's hand.

4. They gradually ascended for half a mile, and then found themselves at the top of a considerable eminence, where the wood ceased, and the eye was instantly caught by Pemberley House, situated on the opposite side of a valley, into which the road with some abruptness wound. It was a large, handsome, stone building, standing well on rising ground, and backed by a ridge of high woody hills;—and in front, a stream of some natural importance was swelled into greater, but without any artificial appearance. Its banks were neither formal, nor falsely adorned. Elizabeth was delighted. She had never seen a place where nature had done more, or where natural beauty had been so little counteracted by an awkward taste. They were all of them warm in her admiration; and at that moment she felt that to be mistress of Pemberley might be something!

These lines open Chapter 43 and provide Elizabeth's introduction to Darcy's grand estate at Pemberley. Her visit to Darcy's home, which occupies a central place in the narrative, operates as a catalyst for her growing attraction toward its owner. In her conversations with the housekeeper, Mrs. Reynolds, Elizabeth hears testimonials of Darcy's wonderful generosity and his kindness as a master; when she encounters Darcy himself, while walking through Pemberley's grounds, he seems altogether changed and his previous arrogance has diminished remarkably. This initial description of the building and grounds at Pemberley serves as a symbol of Darcy's character. The "stream of some natural importance . . . swelled into greater" reminds the reader of his pride, but the fact that it lacks "any artificial appearance" indicates his basic honesty, as does the fact that the stream is neither "formal, nor falsely adorned." Elizabeth's delight, and her sudden epiphany about the pleasure that being mistress of Pemberley must hold, prefigure her later joy in Darcy's continued devotion.

QUOTATIONS

5.   Elizabeth was much too embarrassed to say a word. After a short pause, her companion added, "You are too generous to trifle with me. If your feelings are still what they were last April, tell me so at once. My affections and wishes are unchanged, but one word from you will silence me on this subject forever." Elizabeth feeling all the more than common awkwardness and anxiety of his situation, now forced herself to speak; and immediately, though not very fluently, gave him to understand, that her sentiments had undergone so material a change, since the period to which he alluded, as to make her receive with gratitude and pleasure, his present assurances.

This proposal and Elizabeth's acceptance mark the climax of the novel, occurring in Chapter 58. Austen famously prefers not to stage successful proposals in full, and the reader may be disappointed in the anticlimactic manner in which the narrator relates Elizabeth's acceptance. It is important to remember, however, that the proposal and acceptance are almost a foregone conclusion by this point. Darcy's intervention on behalf of Lydia makes obvious his continuing devotion to Elizabeth, and the shocking appearance of Lady Catherine de Bourgh in the previous chapter, with her haughty attempts to forestall the engagement, serves to suggest strongly that a second proposal from Darcy is imminent.

The clunky language with which the narrator summarizes Elizabeth's acceptance serves a specific purpose, as it captures the one moment of joyful incoherence for this supremely well-spoken character. She accepts Darcy's proposal "immediately," the narrator relates, but "not very fluently." As Elizabeth allows herself to admit that her love has supplanted her long-standing prejudice, her control of language breaks down. The reader is left to imagine, with some delight, the ever-clever Elizabeth fumbling for words to express her irrepressible happiness.

QUOTATIONS

KEY FACTS

FULL TITLE
Pride and Prejudice

AUTHOR
Jane Austen

TYPE OF WORK
Novel

GENRE
Comedy of manners

LANGUAGE
English

TIME AND PLACE WRITTEN
England, between 1796 and 1813

DATE OF FIRST PUBLICATION
1813

PUBLISHER
Thomas Egerton of London

NARRATOR
Third-person omniscient

CLIMAX
Mr. Darcy's proposal to Elizabeth (Volume III, Chapter XVI)

PROTAGONIST
Elizabeth Bennet

ANTAGONIST
Snobbish class-consciousness (epitomized by Lady Catherine de Bourgh and Miss Bingley)

SETTING (TIME)
Some point during the Napoleonic Wars (1797–1815)

SETTING (PLACE)
Longbourn, in rural England

POINT OF VIEW
The novel is primarily told from Elizabeth Bennet's point of view.

FALLING ACTION
The two chapters of the novel after Darcy's proposal

TENSE
Past tense

FORESHADOWING
The only notable example of foreshadowing occurs when Elizabeth visits Pemberley, Darcy's estate, in Volume III, Chapter 1. Her appreciation of the estate foreshadows her eventual realization of her love for its owner.

TONE
Comic—or, in Jane Austen's own words, "light and bright, and sparkling"

THEMES
Love; Reputation; Class

MOTIFS
Courtship; Journeys

SYMBOLS
The novel is light on symbolism, except on the visit to Pemberley, which is described as being "neither formal, nor falsely adorned," and is clearly meant to symbolize the character of Mr. Darcy.

KEY FACTS

STUDY QUESTIONS

1. *Jane Austen's original title for the novel was* FIRST IMPRESSIONS. *What role do first impressions play in Pride and Prejudice?*

Pride and Prejudice is, first and foremost, a novel about surmounting obstacles and achieving romantic happiness. For Elizabeth, the heroine, and Darcy, her eventual husband, the chief obstacle resides in the book's original title: *First Impressions*. Darcy, the proud, prickly noblewoman's nephew, must break free from his original dismissal of Elizabeth as "not handsome enough to tempt me," and from his class-based prejudice against her lack of wealth and family connections. Elizabeth's first impressions, meanwhile, catalogue Darcy as arrogant and self-satisfied; as a result, she later accepts slanderous accusations against him as true.

Both Elizabeth and Darcy are forced to come to grips with their own initial mistakes. Structurally, the first half of the novel traces Darcy's progression to the point at which he is able to admit his love in spite of his prejudice. In the second half, Elizabeth's mistaken impressions are supplanted by informed realizations about Darcy's true character. Darcy's two proposals to Elizabeth chart the mature development of their relationship. He delivers the first at the mid-point of the novel, when he has realized his love for Elizabeth but has not yet escaped his prejudices against her family, and when she is still in the grip of her first, negative impression of him. The second proposal—in which Darcy humbly restates his love for her and Elizabeth, now with full knowledge of Mr. Darcy's good character, happily accepts—marks the arrival of the two characters, each finally achieving the ability to view the other through unprejudiced eyes.

2.   *Analyze how Austen depicts Mr. Bennet. Is he a*
     positive or negative figure?

Mr. Bennet's chief characteristics are an ironic detachment and a sharp, cutting wit. The distance that he creates between himself and the absurdity around him often endears him to the reader and parallels the amused detachment with which Austen treats ridiculous characters such as Mr. Collins and Lady Catherine. To associate the author's point of view with that of Mr. Bennet, however, is to ignore his ultimate failure as a father and husband. He is endlessly witty, but his distance from the events around him makes him an ineffective parent. Detached humor may prove useful for handling the Mr. Collinses of the world, but it is helpless against the depredations of the villainous (but likable) Wickham. When the crisis of Lydia's elopement strikes, Mr. Bennet proves unable to handle the situation. Darcy, decent and energetic, and the Gardiners, whose intelligence, perceptiveness, and resourcefulness make them the strongest adult force in the novel, must step in. He is a likable, entertaining character, but he never manages to earn the respect of the reader.

3. *Discuss the importance of dialogue to character development in the novel.*

All of Austen's many characters come alive through dialogue, as the narrative voice in Austen's work is secondary to the voices of the characters. Long, unwieldy speeches are rare, as are detailed physical descriptions. In their place, the reader hears the crackle of quick, witty conversation. True nature reveals itself in the way the characters speak: Mr. Bennet's emotional detachment comes across in his dry wit, while Mrs. Bennet's hysterical excess drips from every sentence she utters. Austen's dialogue often serves to reveal the worst aspects of her characters—Miss Bingley's spiteful, snobbish attitudes are readily apparent in her words, and Mr. Collins's long-winded speeches (and occasional letters, which are a kind of secondary dialogue) carry with them a tone-deaf pomposity that defines his character perfectly. Dialogue can also conceal bad character traits: Wickham, for instance, hides his rogue's heart beneath the patter of pleasant, witty banter, and he manages to take Elizabeth in with his smooth tongue (although his good looks help as well). Ultimately, though, good conversational ability and general goodness of personality seem to go hand in hand. It is no accident that Darcy and Elizabeth are the best conversationalists in the book: *Pride and Prejudice* is the story of their love, and for the reader, that love unfolds through the words they share.

How to Write
Literary Analysis

The Literary Essay: A Step-by-Step Guide

When you read for pleasure, your only goal is enjoyment. You might find yourself reading to get caught up in an exciting story, to learn about an interesting time or place, or just to pass time. Maybe you're looking for inspiration, guidance, or a reflection of your own life. There are as many different, valid ways of reading a book as there are books in the world.

When you read a work of literature in an English class, however, you're being asked to read in a special way: you're being asked to perform *literary analysis*. To analyze something means to break it down into smaller parts and then examine how those parts work, both individually and together. Literary analysis involves examining all the parts of a novel, play, short story, or poem—elements such as character, setting, tone, and imagery—and thinking about how the author uses those elements to create certain effects.

A literary essay isn't a book review: you're not being asked whether or not you liked a book or whether you'd recommend it to another reader. A literary essay also isn't like the kind of book report you wrote when you were younger, where your teacher wanted you to summarize the book's action. A high school- or college-level literary essay asks, "How does this piece of literature actually work?" "How does it do what it does?" and, "Why might the author have made the choices he or she did?"

The Seven Steps
No one is born knowing how to analyze literature; it's a skill you learn and a process you can master. As you gain more practice with this kind of thinking and writing, you'll be able to craft a method that works best for you. But until then, here are seven basic steps to writing a well-constructed literary essay:

1. *Ask questions*
2. *Collect evidence*
3. *Construct a thesis*

4. Develop and organize arguments
5. Write the introduction
6. Write the body paragraphs
7. Write the conclusion

---

1. ASK QUESTIONS

When you're assigned a literary essay in class, your teacher will often provide you with a list of writing prompts. Lucky you! Now all you have to do is choose one. Do yourself a favor and pick a topic that interests you. You'll have a much better (not to mention easier) time if you start off with something you enjoy thinking about. If you are asked to come up with a topic by yourself, though, you might start to feel a little panicked. Maybe you have too many ideas—or none at all. Don't worry. Take a deep breath and start by asking yourself these questions:

- **What struck you?** Did a particular image, line, or scene linger in your mind for a long time? If it fascinated you, chances are you can draw on it to write a fascinating essay.

- **What confused you?** Maybe you were surprised to see a character act in a certain way, or maybe you didn't understand why the book ended the way it did. Confusing moments in a work of literature are like a loose thread in a sweater: if you pull on it, you can unravel the entire thing. Ask yourself why the author chose to write about that character or scene the way he or she did and you might tap into some important insights about the work as a whole.

- **Did you notice any patterns?** Is there a phrase that the main character uses constantly or an image that repeats throughout the book? If you can figure out how that pattern weaves through the work and what the significance of that pattern is, you've almost got your entire essay mapped out.

- **Did you notice any contradictions or ironies?** Great works of literature are complex; great literary essays recognize and explain those complexities. Maybe the title (*Happy Days*) totally disagrees with the book's subject matter (hungry orphans dying in the woods). Maybe the main character acts one way around his family and a completely different way around his friends and associates. If you can find a way to explain a work's contradictory elements, you've got the seeds of a great essay.

At this point, you don't need to know exactly what you're going to say about your topic; you just need a place to begin your exploration. You can help direct your reading and brainstorming by formulating your topic as a *question,* which you'll then try to answer in your essay. The best questions invite critical debates and discussions, not just a rehashing of the summary. Remember, you're looking for something you can *prove or argue* based on evidence you find in the text. Finally, remember to keep the scope of your question in mind: is this a topic you can adequately address within the word or page limit you've been given? Conversely, is this a topic big enough to fill the required length?

GOOD QUESTIONS

> *"Are Romeo and Juliet's parents responsible for the deaths of their children?"*
>
> *"Why do pigs keep showing up in* LORD OF THE FLIES?*"*
>
> *"Are Dr. Frankenstein and his monster alike? How?"*

BAD QUESTIONS

> *"What happens to Scout in* TO KILL A MOCKINGBIRD?*"*
>
> *"What do the other characters in* JULIUS CAESAR *think about Caesar?"*
>
> *"How does Hester Prynne in* THE SCARLET LETTER *remind me of my sister?"*

---

2. COLLECT EVIDENCE

Once you know what question you want to answer, it's time to scour the book for things that will help you answer the question. Don't worry if you don't know what you want to say yet—right now you're just collecting ideas and material and letting it all percolate. Keep track of passages, symbols, images, or scenes that deal with your topic. Eventually, you'll start making connections between these examples and your thesis will emerge.

Here's a brief summary of the various parts that compose each and every work of literature. These are the elements that you will analyze in your essay, and which you will offer as evidence to support your arguments. For more on the parts of literary works, see the Glossary of Literary Terms at the end of this section.

ELEMENTS OF STORY These are the *what*s of the work—what happens, where it happens, and to whom it happens.

- **Plot:** All of the events and actions of the work.

- **Character:** The people who act and are acted upon in a literary work. The main character of a work is known as the *protagonist.*

- **Conflict:** The central tension in the work. In most cases, the protagonist wants something, while opposing forces (antagonists) hinder the protagonist's progress.

- **Setting:** When and where the work takes place. Elements of setting include location, time period, time of day, weather, social atmosphere, and economic conditions.

- **Narrator:** The person telling the story. The narrator may straightforwardly report what happens, convey the subjective opinions and perceptions of one or more characters, or provide commentary and opinion in his or her own voice.

- **Themes:** The main idea or message of the work—usually an abstract idea about people, society, or life in general. A work may have many themes, which may be in tension with one another.

ELEMENTS OF STYLE These are the *how*s—how the characters speak, how the story is constructed, and how language is used throughout the work.

- **Structure and organization:** How the parts of the work are assembled. Some novels are narrated in a linear, chronological fashion, while others skip around in time. Some plays follow a traditional three- or five-act structure, while others are a series of loosely connected scenes. Some authors deliberately leave gaps in their works, leaving readers to puzzle out the missing information. A work's structure and organization can tell you a lot about the kind of message it wants to convey.

- **Point of view:** The perspective from which a story is told. In *first-person point of view,* the narrator involves him or herself in the story. ("I went to the store"; "We watched in horror as the bird slammed into the window.") A first-person narrator is usually the protagonist of the work, but not always. In *third-person point of view,* the narrator does not participate in the story. A third-person narrator may closely follow a specific character, recounting that individual character's thoughts or experiences, or it may be what we call an *omniscient* narrator. Omniscient narrators see and know all: they can witness any event in any time or place and are privy to the inner thoughts and feelings of all characters. Remember that the narrator and the author are not the same thing!

- **Diction:** Word choice. Whether a character uses dry, clinical language or flowery prose with lots of exclamation points can tell you a lot about his or her attitude and personality.

- **Syntax:** Word order and sentence construction. Syntax is a crucial part of establishing an author's narrative voice. Ernest Hemingway, for example, is known for writing in very short, straightforward sentences, while James Joyce characteristically wrote in long, incredibly complicated lines.

- **Tone:** The mood or feeling of the text. Diction and syntax often contribute to the tone of a work. A novel written in short, clipped sentences that use small, simple words might feel brusque, cold, or matter-of-fact.

- **Imagery:** Language that appeals to the senses, representing things that can be seen, smelled, heard, tasted, or touched.

- **Figurative language:** Language that is not meant to be interpreted literally. The most common types of figurative language are *metaphors* and *similes,* which compare two unlike things in order to suggest a similarity between them— for example, "All the world's a stage," or "The moon is like a ball of green cheese." (Metaphors say one thing *is* another thing; similes claim that one thing is *like* another thing.)

3. Construct a Thesis

When you've examined all the evidence you've collected and know how you want to answer the question, it's time to write your thesis statement. A *thesis* is a claim about a work of literature that needs to be supported by evidence and arguments. The thesis statement is the heart of the literary essay, and the bulk of your paper will be spent trying to prove this claim. A good thesis will be:

- **Arguable.** "*The Great Gatsby* describes New York society in the 1920s" isn't a thesis—it's a fact.

- **Provable through textual evidence**. "*Hamlet* is a confusing but ultimately very well-written play" is a weak thesis because it offers the writer's personal opinion about the book. Yes, it's arguable, but it's not a claim that can be proved or supported with examples taken from the play itself.

- **Surprising**. "Both George and Lenny change a great deal in *Of Mice and Men*" is a weak thesis because it's obvious. A really strong thesis will argue for a reading of the text that is not immediately apparent.

- **Specific**. "Dr. Frankenstein's monster tells us a lot about the human condition" is *almost* a really great thesis statement, but it's still too vague. What does the writer mean by "a lot"? *How* does the monster tell us so much about the human condition?

GOOD THESIS STATEMENTS

Question: In *Romeo and Juliet*, which is more powerful in shaping the lovers' story: fate or foolishness?

Thesis: "Though Shakespeare defines Romeo and Juliet as 'star-crossed lovers' and images of stars and planets appear throughout the play, a closer examination of that celestial imagery reveals that the stars are merely witnesses to the characters' foolish activities and not the causes themselves."

Question: How does the bell jar function as a symbol in Sylvia Plath's *The Bell Jar*?

Thesis: "A bell jar is a bell-shaped glass that has three basic uses: to hold a specimen for observation, to contain gases, and to maintain a vacuum. The bell jar appears in each of these capacities in *The Bell Jar*, Plath's semi-autobiographical novel, and each appearances marks a different stage in Esther's mental breakdown."

Question: Would Piggy in *The Lord of the Flies* make a good island leader if he were given the chance?

Thesis: "Though the intelligent, rational, and innovative Piggy has the mental characteristics of a good leader, he ultimately lacks the social skills necessary to be an effective one. Golding emphasizes this point by giving Piggy a foil in the charismatic Jack, whose magnetic personality allows him to capture and wield power effectively, if not always wisely."

4. Develop and Organize Arguments

The reasons and examples that support your thesis will form the middle paragraphs of your essay. Since you can't really write your thesis statement until you know how you'll structure your argument, you'll probably end up working on steps 3 and 4 at the same time.

There's no single method of argumentation that will work in every context. One essay prompt might ask you to compare and contrast two characters, while another asks you to trace an image through a given work of literature. These questions require different kinds of answers and therefore different kinds of arguments. Below, we'll discuss three common kinds of essay prompts and some strategies for constructing a solid, well-argued case.

Types of Literary Essays

- **Compare and contrast**

> *Compare and contrast the characters of Huck and Jim in* The Adventures of Huckleberry Finn.

Chances are you've written this kind of essay before. In an academic literary context, you'll organize your arguments the same way you would in any other class. You can either go *subject by subject* or *point by point*. In the former, you'll discuss one character first and then the second. In the latter, you'll choose several traits (attitude toward life, social status, images and metaphors associated with the character) and devote a paragraph to each. You may want to use a mix of these two approaches—for example, you may want to spend a paragraph a piece broadly sketching Huck's and Jim's personalities before transitioning into a paragraph or two that describes a few key points of comparison. This can be a highly effective strategy if you want to make a counterintuitive argument—that, despite seeming to be totally different, the two objects being compared are actually similar in a very important way (or vice versa). Remember that your essay should reveal something fresh or unexpected about the text, so think beyond the obvious parallels and differences.

- **Trace**

> *Choose an image—for example, birds, knives, or eyes—and trace that image throughout* Macbeth.

Sounds pretty easy, right? All you need to do is read the play, underline every appearance of a knife in *Macbeth*, and then list them in your essay in the order they appear, right? Well, not exactly. Your teacher doesn't want a simple catalog of examples. He or she wants to see you make *connections* between those examples—that's the difference between summarizing and analyzing. In the *Macbeth* example above, think about the different contexts in which knives appear in the play and to what effect. In *Macbeth,* there are real knives and imagined knives; knives that kill and knives that simply threaten. Categorize and classify your examples to give them some order. Finally, always keep the overall effect in mind. After you choose and analyze your examples, you should come to some greater understanding about the work, as well as your chosen image, symbol, or phrase's role in developing the major themes and stylistic strategies of that work.

- **Debate**

  Is the society depicted in 1984 good for its citizens?

  In this kind of essay, you're being asked to debate a moral, ethical, or aesthetic issue regarding the work. You might be asked to judge a character or group of characters (*Is Caesar responsible for his own demise?*) or the work itself (*Is* JANE EYRE *a feminist novel?*). For this kind of essay, there are two important points to keep in mind. First, don't simply base your arguments on your personal feelings and reactions. Every literary essay expects you to read and analyze the work, so search for evidence in the text. What do characters in *1984* have to say about the government of Oceania? What images does Orwell use that might give you a hint about his attitude toward the government? As in any debate, you also need to make sure that you define all the necessary terms before you begin to argue your case. What does it mean to be a "good" society? What makes a novel "feminist"? You should define your terms right up front, in the first paragraph after your introduction.

  Second, remember that strong literary essays make contrary and surprising arguments. Try to think outside the box. In the *1984* example above, it seems like the obvious answer would be no, the totalitarian society depicted in Orwell's novel is *not* good for its citizens. But can you think of any arguments for the opposite side? Even if your final assertion is that the novel depicts a cruel, repressive, and therefore harmful society, acknowledging and responding to the counterargument will strengthen your overall case.

5. WRITE THE INTRODUCTION

Your introduction sets up the entire essay. It's where you present your topic and articulate the particular issues and questions you'll be addressing. It's also where you, as the writer, introduce yourself to your readers. A persuasive literary essay immediately establishes its writer as a knowledgeable, authoritative figure.

An introduction can vary in length depending on the overall length of the essay, but in a traditional five-paragraph essay it should be no longer than one paragraph. However long it is, your introduction needs to:

- **Provide any necessary context.** Your introduction should situate the reader and let him or her know what to expect. What book are you discussing? Which characters? What topic will you be addressing?

- **Answer the "So what?" question.** Why is this topic important, and why is your particular position on the topic noteworthy? Ideally, your introduction should pique the reader's interest by suggesting how your argument is surprising or otherwise counterintuitive. Literary essays make unexpected connections and reveal less-than-obvious truths.

- **Present your thesis.** This usually happens at or very near the end of your introduction.

- **Indicate the shape of the essay to come.** Your reader should finish reading your introduction with a good sense of the scope of your essay as well as the path you'll take toward proving your thesis. You don't need to spell out every step, but you do need to suggest the organizational pattern you'll be using.

Your introduction should not:

- **Be vague.** Beware of the two killer words in literary analysis: *interesting* and *important*. Of course the work, question, or example is interesting and important—that's why you're writing about it!

- **Open with any grandiose assertions.** Many student readers think that beginning their essays with a flamboyant statement such as, "Since the dawn of time, writers have been fascinated with the topic of free will," makes them sound important and commanding. You know what? It actually sounds pretty amateurish.

- **Wildly praise the work.** Another typical mistake student writers make is extolling the work or author. Your teacher doesn't need to be told that "Shakespeare is perhaps the greatest writer in the English language." You can mention a work's reputation in passing—by referring to *The Adventures of Huckleberry Finn* as "Mark Twain's enduring classic," for example—but don't make a point of bringing it up unless that reputation is key to your argument.

- **Go off-topic.** Keep your introduction streamlined and to the point. Don't feel the need to throw in all kinds of bells and whistles in order to impress your reader—just get to the point as quickly as you can, without skimping on any of the required steps.

---

6. Write the Body Paragraphs

Once you've written your introduction, you'll take the arguments you developed in step 4 and turn them into your body paragraphs. The organization of this middle section of your essay will largely be determined by the argumentative strategy you use, but no matter how you arrange your thoughts, your body paragraphs need to do the following:

- **Begin with a strong topic sentence.** Topic sentences are like signs on a highway: they tell the reader where they are and where they're going. A good topic sentence not only alerts readers to what issue will be discussed in the following paragraph but also gives them a sense of what argument will be made *about* that issue. "Rumor and gossip play an important role in *The Crucible*" isn't a strong topic sentence because it doesn't tell us very much. "The community's constant gossiping creates an environment that allows false accusations to flourish" is a much stronger topic sentence— it not only tells us *what* the paragraph will discuss (gossip) but *how* the paragraph will discuss the topic (by showing how gossip creates a set of conditions that leads to the play's climactic action).

- **Fully and completely develop a single thought.** Don't skip around in your paragraph or try to stuff in too much material. Body paragraphs are like bricks: each individual

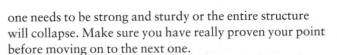

one needs to be strong and sturdy or the entire structure will collapse. Make sure you have really proven your point before moving on to the next one.

- **Use transitions effectively.** Good literary essay writers know that each paragraph must be clearly and strongly linked to the material around it. Think of each paragraph as a response to the one that precedes it. Use transition words and phrases such as *however, similarly, on the contrary, therefore,* and *furthermore* to indicate what kind of response you're making.

---

7. WRITE THE CONCLUSION

Just as you used the introduction to ground your readers in the topic before providing your thesis, you'll use the conclusion to quickly summarize the specifics learned thus far and then hint at the broader implications of your topic. A good conclusion will:

- **Do more than simply restate the thesis.** If your thesis argued that *The Catcher in the Rye* can be read as a Christian allegory, don't simply end your essay by saying, "And that is why *The Catcher in the Rye* can be read as a Christian allegory." If you've constructed your arguments well, this kind of statement will just be redundant.

- **Synthesize the arguments, not summarize them.** Similarly, don't repeat the details of your body paragraphs in your conclusion. The reader has already read your essay, and chances are it's not so long that they've forgotten all your points by now.

- **Revisit the "So what?" question.** In your introduction, you made a case for why your topic and position are important. You should close your essay with the same sort of gesture. What do your readers know now that they didn't know before? How will that knowledge help them better appreciate or understand the work overall?

- **Move from the specific to the general.** Your essay has most likely treated a very specific element of the work—a single character, a small set of images, or a particular passage. In your conclusion, try to show how this narrow discussion has wider implications for the work overall. If your essay on *To Kill a Mockingbird* focused on the character of Boo Radley, for example, you might want to include a bit in your conclusion about how he fits into the novel's larger message about childhood, innocence, or family life.

- **Stay relevant.** Your conclusion should suggest new directions of thought, but it shouldn't be treated as an opportunity to pad your essay with all the extra, interesting ideas you came up with during your brainstorming sessions but couldn't fit into the essay proper. Don't attempt to stuff in unrelated queries or too many abstract thoughts.

- **Avoid making overblown closing statements.** A conclusion should open up your highly specific, focused discussion, but it should do so without drawing a sweeping lesson about life or human nature. Making such observations may be part of the point of reading, but it's almost always a mistake in essays, where these observations tend to sound overly dramatic or simply silly.

A+ Essay Checklist

Congratulations! If you've followed all the steps we've outlined above, you should have a solid literary essay to show for all your efforts. What if you've got your sights set on an A+? To write the kind of superlative essay that will be rewarded with a perfect grade, keep the following rubric in mind. These are the qualities that teachers expect to see in a truly A+ essay. How does yours stack up?

- ✓ Demonstrates a thorough understanding of the book
- ✓ Presents an original, compelling argument
- ✓ Thoughtfully analyzes the text's formal elements
- ✓ Uses appropriate and insightful examples
- ✓ Structures ideas in a logical and progressive order
- ✓ Demonstrates a mastery of sentence construction, transitions, grammar, spelling, and word choice

Suggested Essay Topics

1. *Discuss the importance of social class in the novel, especially as it impacts the relationship between Elizabeth and Darcy.*

2. *Though Jane Austen satirizes snobs in her novels, some critics have accused her of being a snob herself. Giving special consideration to Mrs. Bennet and Mr. Collins, argue and defend one side of this issue.*

3. *Giving special attention to Wickham, Charlotte Lucas, and Elizabeth, compare and contrast male and female attitudes toward marriage in the novel.*

4. *Discuss the relationship between Mrs. Bennet and her children, especially Elizabeth and Lydia.*

5. *Compare and contrast the Bingley-Darcy relationship with the Jane-Elizabeth relationship.*

6. *Compare and contrast the roles of Lady Catherine de Bourgh and Mrs. Bennet.*

A+ STUDENT ESSAY

Many of the female characters in *Pride and Prejudice* feel that women must marry in order to be happy. Does Austen share this view?

Austen's female characters are fixated on marriage, a preoccupation that some modern readers find off-putting. It is true that Austen, like her characters, believes that marriage is the surest route to happiness for women. However, recognizing this state of affairs does not mean she approves of it. *Pride and Prejudice* is not an endorsement of the role of marriage in society; rather, it is a blistering critique of it. Austen stresses the necessity of marriage for women in order to underline how urgently change is needed.

Austen suggests that in her society, love is a desirable component of a marriage, but by no means the most important one. Jane Bennet is ideally suited for Bingley, the man she eventually marries. Yet according to Austen, this compatibility, while wonderful, is almost irrelevant. Far more relevant, from an objective point of view, is the fact that marrying Bingley ensures the fiscal wellbeing of Jane and her family. Jane is the oldest Bennet child, and if she were a man, her father's estate would pass to her upon his death. But the law mandates that the estate pass to Mr. Collins, Mr. Bennet's oldest male relative. As a woman, Jane has only one way to support herself comfortably: by landing a well-off husband. By no means does Austen condone this legal situation. In fact, by making Mr. Collins a buffoon of the first order, she points out how ludicrous it is that Jane must scrabble to find a husband, while a near stranger stands to inherit her beloved father's estate. We can take comfort in Jane's and Bingley's true affection for each other. Austen's key point, however, is that society's backward laws force Jane to choose between marriage and the poorhouse.

Other characters are not as lucky as Jane. Charlotte's marriage to Mr. Collins, one of the more discomfiting unions in Austen's oeuvre, is an implicit criticism of the impossible position in which society puts women. Charlotte does not love Mr. Collins, or even like him very much. Indeed, anyone with a grain of sense would find it hard to tolerate the status-obsessed, self-important clergyman. However, Charlotte cannot justify turning down his proposal. She is six years older than Elizabeth, she has no fortune, and she has no prospective suitors beyond Mr. Collins. Society offers her two choices: She can become an aging spinster with no significant position in society, or she can marry a fool who will provide her with companionship, money, and some status. Neither of these choices is pleasant, but Charlotte decides that the latter is preferable to the former. As she says, "I am not a romantic you know . . . I ask only a comfortable home." With this line of dialogue, Austen makes it clear that for many women, marriage is an unfortunate economic necessity.

Austen emphasizes the absurd strictness of society's attitude toward marriage in Chapters 46 through 49, in which Lydia runs off with Wickham. Austen is less interested in exploring Lydia's experiences—which we hear about only secondhand—than in chronicling the dire impact Lydia's behavior has on her sisters. Society's expectations for marriageable women are so stringent, Austen suggests, that one woman's scandalous behavior is presumed to infect everyone to whom she is related. By sleeping with a man who isn't her husband, Lydia imperils not only her own name, but also the name of her entire family. While the episode ends without disaster, Austen uses it to show the impossible strictness of society's demands on women, and the ease with which reputations can be destroyed and marriage made impossible.

Pride and Prejudice, like Austen's other novels, follows a plot arc that might remind modern readers of light "chick lit" fare. But Austen's emphasis on marriage should never be mistaken for an endorsement of its role in society. Her snappy dialogue and boy-meets-girl plots are merely the pretext for incisive social commentary and challenges to the conventional wisdom.

LITERARY ANALYSIS

GLOSSARY OF LITERARY TERMS

ANTAGONIST

The entity that acts to frustrate the goals of the *protagonist*. The antagonist is usually another *character* but may also be a non-human force.

ANTIHERO / ANTIHEROINE

A *protagonist* who is not admirable or who challenges notions of what should be considered admirable.

CHARACTER

A person, animal, or any other thing with a personality that appears in a *narrative*.

CLIMAX

The moment of greatest intensity in a text or the major turning point in the *plot*.

CONFLICT

The central struggle that moves the *plot* forward. The conflict can be the *protagonist*'s struggle against fate, nature, society, or another person.

FIRST-PERSON POINT OF VIEW

A literary style in which the *narrator* tells the story from his or her own *point of view* and refers to himself or herself as "I." The narrator may be an active participant in the story or just an observer.

HERO / HEROINE

The principal *character* in a literary work or *narrative*.

IMAGERY

Language that brings to mind sense-impressions, representing things that can be seen, smelled, heard, tasted, or touched.

MOTIF

A recurring idea, structure, contrast, or device that develops or informs the major *themes* of a work of literature.

NARRATIVE

A story.

NARRATOR

The person (sometimes a *character*) who tells a story; the *voice* assumed by the writer. The narrator and the author of the work of literature are not the same person.

PLOT

The arrangement of the events in a story, including the sequence in which they are told, the relative emphasis they are given, and the causal connections between events.

POINT OF VIEW

The *perspective* that a *narrative* takes toward the events it describes.

PROTAGONIST

The main *character* around whom the story revolves.

SETTING

The location of a *narrative* in time and space. Setting creates mood or atmosphere.

SUBPLOT

A secondary *plot* that is of less importance to the overall story but may serve as a point of contrast or comparison to the main plot.

SYMBOL

An object, *character,* figure, or color that is used to represent an abstract idea or concept. Unlike an *emblem,* a symbol may have different meanings in different contexts.

SYNTAX

The way the words in a piece of writing are put together to form lines, phrases, or clauses; the basic structure of a piece of writing.

THEME

A fundamental and universal idea explored in a literary work.

TONE

The author's attitude toward the subject or *characters* of a story or poem or toward the reader.

VOICE

An author's individual way of using language to reflect his or her own personality and attitudes. An author communicates voice through *tone, diction,* and *syntax.*

A NOTE ON PLAGIARISM

Plagiarism—presenting someone else's work as your own—rears its ugly head in many forms. Many students know that copying text without citing it is unacceptable. But some don't realize that even if you're not quoting directly, but instead are paraphrasing or summarizing, *it is plagiarism* unless you cite the source.

Here are the most common forms of plagiarism:

- Using an author's phrases, sentences, or paragraphs without citing the source
- Paraphrasing an author's ideas without citing the source
- Passing off another student's work as your own

How do you steer clear of plagiarism? You should *always* acknowledge all words and ideas that aren't your own by using quotation marks around verbatim text or citations like footnotes and endnotes to note another writer's ideas. For more information on how to give credit when credit is due, ask your teacher for guidance or visit www.sparknotes.com.

Review & Resources

Quiz

1. Complete the quotation: "It is a truth universally acknowledged, that a single man in possession of a good fortune, must be in want of a ___."

    A. house
    B. title
    C. wife
    D. dog

2. The Bennet family lives in the village of

    A. Pemberley
    B. Longbourn
    C. Rosings
    D. London

3. Mr. Bingley, when he attends the ball in Meryton, seems to be quite taken with

    A. Elizabeth
    B. Jane
    C. Lydia
    D. Charlotte Lucas

4. How does Mr. Darcy offend Elizabeth at the first ball?

    A. He insults her father.
    B. He dances with Jane too often.
    C. He slaps her.
    D. He refuses to dance with her.

5. Elizabeth's best friend is named

    A. Mrs. Phillips
    B. Charlotte Lucas
    C. Miss Bingley
    D. Mrs. Gardiner

6. Why does Jane's visit to the Bingleys end up lasting for days?

   A. She gets soaked in a rainstorm and becomes ill.
   B. Mr. Bingley proposes to her.
   C. Mrs. Bennet forgets to send a carriage to bring her home.
   D. Jane is hoping to make Mr. Darcy fall in love with her.

7. What does it mean that Mr. Bennet's property is "entailed"?

   A. Lady Catherine de Bourgh gave it to him.
   B. It can only be inherited by a male.
   C. It comes from his wife's family.
   D. He rents from Sir William Lucas.

8. What reason does Wickham give Elizabeth for his dislike of Darcy?

   A. Darcy killed his cousin in a duel.
   B. Darcy wouldn't let Wickham marry his sister.
   C. Darcy betrayed his country.
   D. Darcy cheated him out of an inheritance.

9. To which Bennet daughter does Mr. Collins propose marriage?

   A. Elizabeth
   B. Jane
   C. Mary
   D. Lydia

10. Whom does Mr. Collins marry?

   A. Jane
   B. Lydia
   C. Miss Bingley
   D. Charlotte Lucas

11. Why does Miss Bingley dislike Elizabeth?

    A. She is jealous of Darcy's growing attraction to Elizabeth.

    B. Elizabeth insulted Miss Bingley at the ball.

    C. Wickham has told Miss Bingley lies about Elizabeth's character.

    D. Darcy is constantly speaking ill of Elizabeth.

12. Where do the Bingleys and Darcy go for the winter?

    A. Pemberley

    B. London

    C. They remain at Netherfield

    D. France

13. In March, Elizabeth goes to visit

    A. Miss Darcy

    B. Charlotte Lucas

    C. Wickham and Lydia

    D. Miss Bingley

14. Lady Catherine de Bourgh is Darcy's

    A. Aunt

    B. Sister

    C. Mother

    D. First wife

15. When Darcy first proposes to Elizabeth, he spends most of the proposal dwelling on

    A. Her beauty

    B. How socially unsuitable a match she is for him

    C. How much he adores her family

    D. How much money he will lavish on her

16. When Darcy proposes for the first time, Elizabeth

    A. Tells him that she is engaged to Wickham

    B. Asks him for more time

    C. Turns him down

    D. Faints

REVIEW & RESOURCES

17. Elizabeth's feelings toward Darcy begin to change when he

    A. Sends her a letter explaining his actions
    B. Fights a duel with Wickham
    C. Sends money to Jane
    D. Marries Miss Bingley

18. Darcy's estate is called

    A. Rosings
    B. London
    C. Pemberley
    D. Brighton

19. Where does Lydia spend the summer, and why?

    A. Netherfield, to be near Darcy
    B. London, because she enjoys the opera
    C. Brighton, to be near the militia regiment
    D. Barbados, for her health

20. What socially disastrous romantic decision does Lydia make?

    A. She elopes with Wickham.
    B. She marries Bingley.
    C. She rejects Mr. Collins's proposal.
    D. She runs away to France with a lover.

21. Who spearheads the search for Lydia after Mr. Bennet returns home in defeat?

    A. Mr. Gardiner
    B. Sir William Lucas
    C. Charlotte Lucas
    D. Mrs. Phillips

22. Who pays off Wickham, convincing him to marry Lydia?

    A. Bingley
    B. Darcy
    C. Mr. Gardiner
    D. Mr. Collins

23. When he returns to Netherfield, Mr. Bingley

    A.   Has just married Miss Darcy
    B.   Pursues the priesthood
    C.   Begins courting Elizabeth
    D.   Resumes courting Jane

24. What does Lady Catherine forbid Elizabeth to do?

    A.   Marry Bingley
    B.   Visit Rosings
    C.   Marry Darcy
    D.   See Wickham

25. The novel ends with

    A.   Darcy marrying Elizabeth, and Bingley marrying Miss Darcy
    B.   Darcy marrying Elizabeth, and Wickham marrying Jane
    C.   Bingley marrying Jane, and Elizabeth marrying Wickham
    D.   Bingley marrying Jane, and Darcy marrying Elizabeth

SUGGESTIONS FOR FURTHER READING

BLOOM, HAROLD, ed. *Jane Austen's* PRIDE AND PREJUDICE: *Modern Critical Interpretations.* New York: Chelsea House Publishers, 2007.

BUSH, DOUGLAS. *Jane Austen.* New York: Macmillan Publishing, 1975.

BUTLER, MARILYN. *Jane Austen and the War of Ideas.* Oxford: Oxford University Press, reprint eition 2002.

EMSLEY, SARAH. *Jane Austen's Philosophy of the Virtues.* New York: Palgrave Macmillan, 2005.

GILBERT, SANDRA and SUSAN GUBAR. *The Madwoman in the Attic: The Woman Writer and the 19th Century Literary Imagination.* New Haven, CT: Yale University Press, reprint edition 2000.

HONAN, PARK. *Jane Austen: Her Life.* New York: St. Martin's Press, reprint edition, 1996.

LASKI, MARGARET. *Jane Austen and Her World.* Norwich, England: Thames and Hudson, 1977.

MORRISON, ROBERT. *Jane Austen's* PRIDE & PREJUDICE: *A Sourcebook.* New York: Routledge, 2005.

ROSS, JOSEPHINE. *Jane Austen: A Companion.* Piscataway, NJ: Rutgers University Press, 2003.